Improving
learning ability
through
compensatory
physical education

Improving learning ability through compensatory physical education

By **JAMES H. HUMPHREY**

Professor of Physical Education and
Motor Activity Learning Specialist
University of Maryland
College Park, Maryland

With a Foreword by

Betty H. Simms

Professor of Special Education
University of Maryland
College Park, Maryland

CHARLES C THOMAS • **PUBLISHER**
Springfield • Illinois • U. S. A.

Published and Distributed Throughout the World by

CHARLES C THOMAS • PUBLISHER

Bannerstone House

301-327 East Lawrence Avenue, Springfield, Illinois, U.S.A.

Printed in the United States of America

R-1

Library of Congress Cataloging in Publication Data

Humphrey, James Harry, 1911-
    Improving learning ability through compensatory
physical education.

    Includes indexes.
    1. Perceptual-motor learning.   2. Slow learning
children.   I. Title.
LB1067.H85   371.9′044   76-12409
ISBN 0-398-03561-X

FOREWORD

M ANY books and articles have been written about physical education and about children with special learning needs. This book combines an examination of those children's needs with a rationale for teachers to provide a compensatory physical education program.

Professor Humphrey is an established educator, internationally known for both his research and his practical knowledge in the field of physical education. Both forms of his contributions appear in this book. However, it contains more than an analysis of research findings related to developing perceptual-motor skills in children with special needs and also more than well thought out designs for teachers. It is a book which conveys the author's enthusiasm for providing developmental experiences for children in relaxed and natural activities. Throughout this work there is a link between scientific research and practical suggestions for teaching children.

Its purpose is to offer teachers a resource to stimulate thinking consistent with the current emphasis on individual differences, and to provide them with specific suggestions which will contribute to good teaching for children with underdeveloped skills in perceptual-motor areas. With this resource a teacher can select activities which will facilitate learning and enhance the learner's self-concept.

The text is both interpretive and practical. A review of research related to sensory processing and neural and anatomical aspects of movement directs attention to the development of physical abilities in children who may have developmental delays because of central nervous system dysfunction or social and emotional problems. There is information stressing the identification of learning problems through observation and testing, and, most important, the description of a series of carefully designed and selected activities which can be used to alleviate the problems. There is an emphasis on the use of assessment to evaluate various phases of the learning situations. The content is a timely contribution in response to the current educational thrust to identify individual needs, and to provide experiences which will correct or improve perceptual-motor competencies in children with potential to learn.

The distinctive theme of this book is that carefully selected physical activities — child-oriented games, rhythmic activities, and self-testing activities — can be used as learning-to-learn experiences. Physical education activities, free from pressure and stress for children with special needs, can be used to develop body image and self-awareness, laterality and sense of direction, kinesthetic and tactile perception skills, and auditory and visual perception skills. Special concern is given to the interpretation of compensatory physical education which can be directed toward improving the learning abilities of children within the total educational program. It is a sequentially organized program of interesting and motivating physical education activities for children who need opportunities to develop specific skills, especially in the fine motor areas. Also, the value of physical education experiences in the lives of children to build self-awareness, self-concept and self-evaluation skills should be explored by all teachers. Compensatory physical education provides a natural motivation for learning at all levels for all ages.

BETTY H. SIMMS

PREFACE

THE term "compensatory physical education" is perhaps new to most people. I first introduced the term to the literature in early 1974, having derived it from the manner in which some British writers have used the term "compensatory education." That is, they have used the term "compensatory education" to connote an attempt to make good certain deficiencies in a person's earlier education — with specific reference to perceptual-motor deficiencies. The insertion of the word "physical" indicates that the attempt to improve such deficiencies will take place through the *physical* aspect of personality. Thus, compensatory physical education is a branch of physical education which purports to correct or improve upon perceptual-motor deficiences through participation in regular physical education activities, as compared to the use of structured perceptual-motor programs for this purpose. The intent of the present text is to explore this possibility and make recommendations for its use and implementation.

The reader should understand that practically any movement experience will involve some aspect of perceptual-motor development. Therefore, the activities suggested in the book merely scratch the surface of the almost unlimited possibilities. In other words, various representative examples have been provided and can serve as a starting point for expansion by creative teachers. It also should be clearly understood that there is a great deal of overlapping as far as perceptual-motor developmental factors are concerned. All these factors are inextricably interwoven, interrelated and interdependent upon each other. This, of course, makes it difficult to classify activities with reference to a specific area of perceptual-motor development. While an attempt has been made in this direction, many of the activities could be placed in more than one classification with satifactory results accruing.

The first three chapters take into account the nature, function and philosophy of compensatory physical education as conceived by the author. Chapters 4 through 7 get into specific physical education activities in such areas as body concept, laterality and directionality, kinesthetic and tactile perception, and visual and auditory perception. The final chapter deals with possible ways and means of developing and implementing compensatory physical education programs.

The book should serve a variety of uses. It could serve as a basic text in those professional preparation courses oriented to the improvement of learning ability of children. It could find use in courses involving the use of perceptual-motor development in physical education. Finally, it should serve as a valuable reference book of resources for teachers who, in some way, deal with the learning disability problems of children.

The activities that appear in the book, over 175 in number, have undergone extensive field trials in various situations, and I am indebted to the many teachers who took part in these endeavors. I also wish to extend grateful acknowledgment to Dr. Betty H. Simms, Professor of Special Education at the University of Maryland, who evaluated the material from the point of view of the specialist in learning disability and prepared the foreword.

JAMES H. HUMPHREY

CONTENTS

Improving
learning ability
through
compensatory
physical education

Chapter 1

THE NATURE OF COMPENSATORY PHYSICAL EDUCATION

IN the mid-1970s I introduced to the literature a classification which divided the broad area of elementary school physical education into three different branches. The arbitrary terminology used to describe these three branches with *curricular* physical education, *cognitive* physical education, and *compensatory* physical education.[1] Although each branch is conceived as a separate entity, there is obvious overlapping between the branches. The reason for this, of course, is that the basic and underlying concept in the utilization of physical education experiences is the same in any situation. That is, these experiences are oriented in various degrees of physical, social, emotional, and intellectual development of children.

The thrust of this volume is concerned with *compensatory* physical education. However, in order to put compensatory physical education into proper perspective it appears imperative at the outset to describe each of these branches.

CURRICULAR PHYSICAL EDUCATION

This basic branch implies that physical education should be a subject in the elementary school curriculum in the same manner that mathematics is a subject, or science is a subject, and so on. Such factors as sufficient facilities, adequate time allotment, and above all, good teaching, should be provided to carry out the most desirable physical education learning experiences for children. A curriculum that is child-oriented and scientifically developed should be provided as would be the case with the language arts curriculum or the social studies curriculum or any other curriculum in the school. It is in this branch that the child should learn

[1] James H. Humphrey, *Child Learning Through Elementary School Physical Education*, 2nd ed. (Dubuque, Iowa, Wm. C. Brown, 1974): p. 6-10.

3

to move efficiently and effectively and to learn the various kinds of motor skills. This should include locomotor skills, auxiliary skills and skills of propulsion and retrieval needed for satisfactory performance in game activities, rhythmic activities and self-testing activities.

Two natural subclassifications of curricular physical education could be *adapted* physical education and *extraclass* physical education. The term "adapted" means that special kinds of activities are adapted for use with children who have some sort of physical impairment. An extraclass program, consisting of the two broad categories of *intramural* activities (within the school) and *interscholastic* activities (between schools), if conducted at all, should be a natural outgrowth of the regular curricular physical education class program.

COGNITIVE PHYSICAL EDUCATION

This branch of physical education, which considers its use as a learning medium in other curriculum areas, might well be considered by some as a relatively recent innovation. In essence, cognitive physical education involves the selection of a physical education activity in which a specific skill or concept of a subject area has a relatively high degree of inherency. The physical education activity is taught to the children and used as a learning medium to develop the skill or concept in the specific subject area. It is theorized that a concept becomes a part of the child's physical reality as the child participates in the activity where the concept is inherent. An example of such an activity follows:

The concept to be developed is the science concept *electricity travels along a pathway and needs a complete circuit over which to travel*. A physical education activity in which this concept is inherent is *straddle ball roll*.

The children stand one behind the other in relay files with six to ten children in each file. All are in a side stride position with feet far enough apart so that a ball can be rolled between the legs of the players. The first person in each file holds a rubber playground ball. At a signal, the person at the front of each file starts the activity by attempting to roll the ball between the legs of all of the players on his team. The team which moves the ball in the manner described to the last member of its file first, scores a point. The last player goes to the head of his file and this procedure is continued with a point scored each time for the team which moves the ball back to the last player first. After every player has had an opportunity to roll the ball back, the team scoring the most points is declared the winner.

In applying this activity to develop the concept, the first player at the head of each file becomes the electric switch which opens and shuts the circuit. The ball is the electric current. As the ball rolls between the children's legs, it moves right through if all of the legs are properly lined up. When a leg is not in the proper stride, the path of the ball is impeded and the ball rolls out. The activity has to be stopped until the ball is recovered and the correction made in the position of the leg. The circuit has to be repaired (the child's leg) before the flow of electricity (the roll of the ball) can be resumed.

Cognitive physical education should be considered as only *one* aspect of physical education and not the major purpose of it. We should consider curricular physical education as a subject in its own right. Consequently, the use of physical education as a learning medium in other subject areas ordinarily should not occur during the regular time allotted to physical education. On the contrary, this approach should be considered a learning activity in the same way that other kinds of learning activities are used in a given subject area. This means, that for the most part, this procedure should be used during the time allotted to the particular subject area in question. Moreover, the classroom teacher would ordinarily do the teaching when this approach is used. The function of the physical education teacher would be to work closely with the classroom teacher and furnish him or her with suitable physical education activities to use in the development of concepts. This is to say that the classroom teacher is familiar with the skills and concepts to be developed, and similarly the physical education teacher should know those activities that could be used to develop the skills and concepts.

COMPENSATORY PHYSICAL EDUCATION

The term *compensatory* as it applies to education is not new, and over the years it has been used in a variety of ways. Possibly its derivation dates back to mid-nineteenth century Denmark.[2] At that time, what was known as the "compensatory education of cripples" involved the teaching of boys and young men with certain physical impairments such skills as basketmaking and shoemaking. The purpose was to prepare people who had certain deformities to be able to make a living on their own.

In this country at about the turn of the century it was reported that "by compensatory education for deformed children is meant any special training which will make amends for their physical shortcomings and convert little cripples into men and women better fitted in some one direction to cope with fellow-man in the struggle for life."[3]

In recent years in this country compensatory education has taken on a much different meaning. That is, it has been concerned essentially with "compensating" for an inadequate early education in some way, or providing a better background for beginning schoolchildren who come from a low socioeconomic background. A case in point is the *Headstart* program sponsored by the federal government.

More recently, educators and psychologists in Great Britain have attached still a different meaning to compensatory education.[4] In this regard Morris and Whiting have indicated that the term *compensatory education* now being used tends to replace the former term *re-education*. They contend that the term *re-education* was often misused when standing for compensatory education. Re-education implied educating again persons who had previously reached an educational level and who now, for some reason did not exhibit behavior at a level of which they were previously capable. These authors assert that compensatory education implies an attempt to make good a deficiency in a person's earlier education, and give as examples of this some of the structured perceptual-motor training programs that have originated

---

[2]The Education of Crippled Children, *American Physical Education Review*, vol. III, no. 3 (September, 1898): p. 190-191.
[3]The Education of Crippled Children, *American Physical Education Review*.
[4]P. R. Morris and H. T. A. Whiting, *Motor Impairment and Compensatory Education*, (Philadelphia, Lea & Febiger, 1971): p. 9.

in the United States. Specifically mentioned in this connection are the Frostig approach[5] and the Kephart approach.[6]

It is from this source that the author derived the term *compensatory physical education.* The rationale for this term is that ordinarily the attempts to improve a deficiency in one's earlier education is likely to take place through the *physical* aspect of the individual's personality. Whereas the standard structured perceptual-motor training programs purport to improve learning ability through systematic exercises and procedures, compensatory physical education, as conceived here, seeks to improve upon learning ability through participation in regular physical education activities. At this point it seems appropriate to point out that compensatory physical education should not be confused with what has been called *corrective* physical education or *adapted* physical education. The former has been used to correct certain physical impairments (flat feet, round shoulders, etc.) while the latter means that the physical education program is adapted to meet the needs of those individuals who have certain health anomalies.

While compensatory physical education and cognitive physical education are essentially based on the same concept, the manner in which these two approaches are used should not be confused. It could be said that compensatory physical education is essentially concerned with education *of* the physical, while cognitive physical education is concerned with education *through* the physical.

Compensatory physical education attempts to correct various types of child learning disabilities which may stem from an impairment of the central nervous system and/or have their roots in certain social or emotional problems of children. This branch of physical education, most often through the medium of *perceptual-motor development,* involves the correction, or at least some degree of improvement, of certain motor deficiencies,

[5]Marianne Frostig Center of Educational Therapy. (This center is under the direction of Marianne Frostig and devotes its services to children with learning disabilities.)
[6]Glenhaven Achievement Center. (This center was under the direction of the late Dr. Newell C. Kephart, one of the early exponents of perceptual-motor training for children with learning disabilities.)

especially those associated with fine coordination. What some specialists have identified as a "perceptual-motor deficit" syndrome is said to exist with certain neurologically handicapped children. An attempt may be made to correct or improve fine motor control problems through a carefully developed sequence of motor competencies which follow a definite hierarchy of development. This may occur through the structured perceptual-motor program which is likely to be dependent upon a series of systematic physical exercises. Or, it can occur through compensatory physical education which attempts to provide for these corrections or improvement by having children engage in physical education activities where perceptual-motor developmental factors may be inherent. This procedure tends to be much more fun for children and at the same time is more likely to be free from emotionally traumatizing situations sometimes attendant in some structured perceptual-motor programs. In this regard a recent comment by Dauer and Pagrazi[7] is of interest.

> An effective physical education program will include in its normal format all of the movement elements inherent in perceptual-motor competency and these elements are an important part of a very good physical education program and provide benefit for all children, particularly those in the lower grades. If the children have these experiences within the physical education program there is little need to structure a separate perceptual-motor program or to substitute such a program for normal physical education activities for children.

The advantage of compensatory physical education is that it can be incorporated into the regular physical education program rather easily. It can be a part of the function of the physical education teacher, and, with assistance, the classroom teacher can handle many aspects of compensatory physical education.

The foregoing statements should not be misinterpreted as excessive criticism of structured perceptual-motor programs. Under certain conditions, and perhaps particularly in cases of severe neurological dysfunction, such programs can be useful. However, caution and restraint in the use of highly structured

---

[7]Victor P. Dauer and Robert P. Pangrazi, *Dynamic Physical Education for Elementary School Children,* 5th ed. (Minneapolis, Burgess Publishing Company, 1975): p. 149.

perceptual-motor training should be exercised and these programs should be conducted under adequate supervision and by properly prepared personnel.

Children Who Can Benefit from Compensatory Physical Education

We need to take into account the type of child who can receive the most satisfactory benefits from compensatory physical education. Ordinarily, those children who have certain problems in learning are placed in the broad category of slow learners. One classification of slow learners is (1) children with mental retardation, (2) children with depressed potential, and (3) children with learning disabilities. It is the third classification — children with learning disabilities — with which compensatory physical education is most vitally concerned.

Since classroom achievement of children with learning disabilities may be similar to those children who suffer from mental retardation and depressed potential, the problem of identification is of utmost importance. Johnson and Myklebust warn of the imperative need of proper identification of these children: "Often the child with a learning disability is labeled slow or lazy when in reality he is neither. These labels have an adverse effect on future learning, on self-perception and on feelings of personal worth."[8]

The research identifying children with learning disabilities indicates that their achievement has been impaired in specific areas of both verbal and/or nonverbal learning, but their *potential* for learning is categorized as normal or above. Thus, these children with learning disabilities fall within the 90 and above IQ range in either the verbal or nonverbal areas. Total IQ is not used as the criterion for determining learning potential inasmuch as adequate intelligence (either verbal or nonverbal) may be obscured in cases where the total IQ falls below 90, but in which specific aspects of intelligence fall within the definition of adequate intelligence. The child whose IQ falls below the normal

---

[8]Doris J. Johnson and Helmer R. Myklebust, *Learning Disabilities* (New York, Grune & Stratton, 1967): p. 49.

range and who has a learning disability is considered to have a multiple involvement.

A child with a learning disability has deficits in verbal and/or nonverbal learning. There may be impairment of expressive, receptive, or integrative functions. There is concern for deficits in the function of input and output, of sensory modalities and overloading, and of degree of impairment. The essential differences between the mentally retarded person and the child with a learning disability have been characterized as the following:

> One cannot deny that the neurology of learning has been disturbed in the mentally retarded, but the fundamental effect has been to reduce potential for learning in general. Though some retarded children have isolated *high* levels of function, the pattern is one of generalized inferiority; normal potential for learning is *not* assumed. In comparison, children with learning disabilities have isolated *low* levels of function. The pattern is one of generalized integrity of mental capacity; normal potential *is* assumed.[9]

Consequently, the child with a learning disability shows marked differences from the child with limited potential. There are both qualitative and quantitative differences. This child has more potential for learning, and the means by which he learns are different.

While there may be some overlapping in the educational methods used with the groups identified as slow learners, there obviously must be differentiation in educational goals and approaches for these various groups. Correct identification of the factors causing slowness in learning is essential in teaching to the individual differences of children. The theories and practices labeled as compensatory physical education, outline an effective approach for teachers working with the child appropriately identified as one with learning disabilities.

Some Objective Support for Compensatory Physical Education

As far back as the late 1960s some writers were commenting on

---

[9]Doris J. Johnson and Helmer R. Myklebust, *Learning Disabilities*, (New York, Grune & Stratton, 1967): p. 55.

the inherency of perceptual-motor activities in many physical education experiences. Notable among these proponents was Dr. Hope M. Smith, Professor of Physical Education at Purdue University.[10]

She indicated that most experiences employed in perceptual-motor training programs were also found in good elementary school programs of physical education. She suggested programs involving balancing activities, self-testing activities, rhythmic activities, and games and relays. She also noted that activities and experiences which should comprise elementary school physical education programs have long been of concern to physical educators. And further, that in their attempts to design these programs they have suffered from the same lack that has plagued proponents of the current programs for children with learning disabilities. That is, objective evidence that would guide one in providing the most effective experiences for the *optimum duration,* at the *appropriate intensity,* and in the *best sequence* to achieve the purposes of the program.

In recent years various studies have ameliorated this condition somewhat. Some representative examples of these studies follow:

In a study by Davis[11] the purpose was to investigate the effects of a perceptually-oriented physical education program (PPE) on perceptual-motor ability and academic ability of kindergarten and first grade children. Also investigated was the relationship between perceptual-motor ability and academic ability of these two grade levels. The study consisted of two parts. Part one dealt with the effects of the PPE program on kindergarten subjects. Three classes of kindergarten children were randomly divided into four groups. Three of these groups received varying amounts of the PPE program while the fourth group acted as a control and received no PPE. One of the three PPE groups received the PPE program one time a week for 25 minutes; another received it two times a week for 25 minutes; and the third received it for 25

[10]Hope M. Smith, "Motor Activity and Perceptual Development: Some Implications for Physical Education," *Journal of Health, Physical Education and Recreation, vol. 39,* February 1968, p. 29.
[11]Robert G. Davis, "The Effect of Perceptually Oriented Physical Education on Perceptual-Motor Ability and Academic Ability of Kindergarten and First Grade Children," Doctoral Dissertation, University of Maryland, College Park, Maryland, 1973.

minutes three times a week.

The second part of the study dealt with the effect of the same PPE program administered to the kindergarten subjects on first grade children. Four classes of first grade subjects were randomly divided into four groups with three groups receiving the PPE program while the fourth group acted as a control and received no PPE. One of the first grade PPE groups met for two 20-minute periods per week; another met for two 30-minute periods and the third met for two 40-minute periods.

The training lasted for 15 weeks for both grade levels. The ABC Inventory and the Dayton Sensory Motor Awareness Survey for four and five-year olds were used to evaluate the effects of the PPE program on the kindergarten children. The Boehm Test of Basic Concepts and the Purdue Perceptual-Motor Survey were used to evaluate the effect of the PPE program on the first grade subjects. A statistical analysis of the data revealed that there were no significant differences among the groups at either grade level on academic ability following the PPE program. No significant differences were found in the kindergarten children's perceptual-motor ability following the PPE program. A significant difference in perceptual-motor ability was found, however, between the three first grade groups that received the PPE program and the control group, in favor of the PPE groups. The results of the study warranted the generalization that perceptually-oriented physical education would appear of value for increasing perceptual-motor ability at the first grade level.

In another study patterned generally along the same lines as Davis's study, Richmond[12] compared *individualized* physical education activities with *group* physical education activities for the development of perceptual-motor skills in first grade children.

All of the first grade children in one of the elementary schools in Baltimore, Maryland were randomly assigned to one of two groups and assigned one of the two treatments. The first group

[12]Clement L. Richmond, "A Comparison of Individualized Physical Education Activities with Group Physical Education Activities for the Development of Perceptual-Motor Skills in First Grade Children," Masters Thesis, University of Maryland, College Park, Maryland, 1973.

was assigned a program of physical education utilizing group activities which emphasized the development of perceptual-motor skills. The second group was assigned an individual program of physical education which also emphasized the development of perceptual-motor skills. The Boehm Test was used to assess academic ability, and the Purdue Perceptual-Motor Survey was used to measure perceptual-motor ability.

The study was carried out three days a week for a period of eight weeks, at which time a post-test was administered. A statistical analysis indicated that each group gained equally from pretest to post-test on both criterion tests. There was no significant difference between the two groups on either measure. The results of this study differed from that of Davis in that both groups showed gain in academic ability as well as in perceptual-motor ability. It was generalized that both individual and group physical education activities could be used to improve perceptual-motor ability and academic ability of first grade children.

In the final study reported here, Schwab[13] compared the effects of Frostig Move-Grow-Learn Activities and selected active games on the improvement of reading readiness in first grade children.

A total of ninety-three first grade children were given the Primary Mental Abilities Test K-1 in perceptual speed and spacial relations. They were randomly divided into a group which received the Frostig program, a second group which received an active games program in which the variables studied were inherent, and a third group which received classroom instruction in reading readiness along with the regular physical education program. After a six-week training program a post-test was administered. The results showed that there were no significant differences between the three groups. It was generalized that either of the three procedures would be acceptable for use in improving reading readiness of first grade children. Observers noted that the active games group seemed to be more motivated and at the same time appeared to receive a greater amount of enjoyment from the learning experience than did the other two groups.

---

[13]Joy Green Schwab, "A Comparison of the Effects of Frostig Move-Grow-Learn Activities and Selected Active Games on the Improvement of Reading Readiness in First Grade Children," Masters Thesis, University of Maryland, College Park, Maryland, 1973.

I should point out very forcefully that the research in this area does not provide data that is extensive enough to carve a clear-cut profile. However, the data are suggestive enough to give rise to some interesting generalizations and speculations regarding the value of compensatory physical education as an important medium in improving the learning ability of children. It will remain the responsibility of further research to provide more conclusive evidence to support these speculations. There is hope, however, based on actual practical experience with this approach, to encourage those responsible for improving and facilitating learning for children with learning disabilities to join in the collection of further evidence to verify the contribution of compensatory physical education to the educational curriculum.

Chapter 2

PERCEPTUAL-MOTOR DEVELOPMENT

PERCEPTION is concerned with how we obtain information from the environment through the various sensory modalities and what we make of it. In the present context the term *motor* is concerned with the impulse for motion resulting in a change of position through the various forms of body movement. Espenschade[1] suggests that when the two terms are put together (perceptual-motor) the implication is an organization of interpretation of sensory data, with related voluntary motor responses.

PERCEPTUAL-MOTOR SKILLS

There is a considerable amount of agreement among child development specialists that there is no simple distinction between a perceptual skill and a motor skill. This has, no doubt, led to the term *perceptual-motor skills*. In fact, to some extent this term seems to be supplanting such terms as *neuromuscular* and *sensorimotor*.

In general, the current postulation appears to be that if perceptual training improves perceptual and motor abilities, then, because of the fact that perceptual and motor abilities are so highly interrelated and interdependent upon each other, it follows that training in perception should alleviate perceptual-motor problems. There is abundant objective support for the notion that perception training can improve perceptual ability. Although there is not a great deal of clear-cut evidence to support the idea that perceptual-motor training does increase the performance ability in perceptual-motor skills, some research, such as the work of Johnson and Fretz[2] has indicated that certain of perceptual-motor skills can be significantly improved for certain

[1]Anna S. Espenschade, "Perceptual-Motor Development in Children," *The Academy Papers*, no. 1, *The American Academy of Physical Education*, 1968, pp. 14-22.
[2]Warren R. Johnson and Bruce R. Fretz, "Changes in Perceptual-Motor Skills After a Children's Physical Development Program," *Perceptual and Motor Skills*, April 1967.

children who take part in a physical development program for a specified period of time.

What then are the perceptual-motor skills? Generally, the kinds of skills that fit into a combination of manual coordinations and eye-hand skills may be considered a valid classification.

Visual perception is based on sensorimotor experiences that depend on visual acuity, eye-hand coordination, left-right body orientation, and other visual-spatial abilities, including visual sequencing.

Studies have shown a positive correlation between difficulties in visual perception and achievement in reading. Strang cites numerous studies in concluding that, "In general, average and superior readers tend to perform better than retarded readers on tests of perceptual differentiation, tests of closure, and measures of lag in perceptual-motor maturation."[3]

Indications of a child's eye-hand coordination may be observed as he bounces or throws a ball, erases a chalkboard, cuts paper with scissors, copies a design, ties his shoe laces, picks up small objects from the floor, or replaces a cap on a pen. It has been indicated that in reading, the child shows difficulty in eye-hand coordination by his inability to keep his place in reading, to find the place again in the pattern of printed words, and to maintain the motor adjustment as long as is necessary to comprehend word, phrase, or sentence. His tendency to skip lines arises from an inability to direct his eyes accurately to the beginning of the next line.[4]

Depending upon a variety of extenuating circumstances, perceptual-motor skills require various degrees of voluntary action. The basic striking and catching skills are examples of this type and are important in certain kinds of active game activities; that is, receiving an object (catching) such as a ball, and hitting (striking) an object, ordinarily with an implement, such as batting a ball. Other kinds of skills in this category, but not related to game activities, include sorting of objects, finger painting, and bead stringing. There is another group of tasks perceptual-motor

---

[3]Ruth Strang, *Diagnostic Teaching of Reading*, 2nd ed. (New York, McGraw-Hill Book Company, 1969): p. 153.
[4]Ruth Strang, *Diagnostic Teaching of Reading*.

in nature which involve such factors as choice, discrimination, and problem solving. These may be uncovered by various types of intelligence tests and the ability to perform the tasks under certain conditions.

There are tasks, perceptual-motor in character, that are accomplished with one hand. At a high level of performance this could involve receiving a ball with one hand in a highly organized sports activity such as baseball. At a very low level, a baby will reach for an object or grasp an object with one hand.

In some kinds of visual tasks requiring the use of one eye, there appears to be an eye preference. In reading, it is believed that one eye may lead or be dominant. In tasks where one eye is used and one hand is used, most people will use those on the same side of the body. This is to say that there is *lateral dominance.* In the case of those who use the left eye and right hand or the opposite of this, *mixed dominance* is said to exist. Some studies suggest that mixed dominance may have a negative effect on motor coordination, but perhaps just as many investigators report that this is not the case.

Masland and Cratty have summarized the research on the relationship between handedness, brain dominance, and reading ability, and characterize the research as voluminous, often contradictory, and most confusing.[5] The following conclusions are based on their broad review of the research:

1. It has not been demonstrated that laterality of hand or eye dominance or mixed dominance bear a direct relationship to poor reading.
2. There is a very low correlation between handedness or eyedness and brain dominance for language. There is no evidence that changing handedness will influence the lateralization of other functions.
3. There are neither theoretical nor empirical data to support efforts to change handedness or eyedness as a means of improving reading ability.

A condition often related to dominance as far as reading is

---

[5]Richard L. Masland and Bryant J. Cratty, "The Nature of the Reading Process, the Rational Non-educational Remedial Methods," Eloise O. Calkins, ed. *Reading Forum*, NIMDS Monograph no. 11, Department of Health, Education and Welfare, Washington, D. C.

concerned is that of *reversals*. One type of reversal (static) refers to a child seeing letters reversed such as *n* and *b* appearing as *u* and *d*. In another type (kinetic) the child may see the word *no* as *on*. At one time reversals were considered as possibly related to dominance. However, later studies tended to negate this earlier view. In more recent years studies tend to support the contention that problems of visual perception, spatial orientation, and recognition of form rather than dominance patterns result in children making reversals.

Perhaps some mention should be made regarding the most satisfactory ways of presenting perceptual-motor skills to children. Although a great deal of evidence has not been accumulated to support one method over another, the work of Smith[6] is of interest.

The purpose of this study was to determine the extent to which kindergarten children were ready for first grade experiences, and to attempt to compare the effects of three methods of presenting perceptual-motor skills on the reading readiness of randomly placed kindergarten children. The results indicated that there was no significant difference between the direct and problem-solving methods of teaching these skills. However, there was a greater mean score gain in the combined directed *and* problem-solving groups when compared with a group where color coded targets were used rather than verbalized directions for the movements. Thus, it was generalized that just doing the movement will not bridge all perceptual-motor learning gaps. It appeared that there is a greater understanding and transfer of learning if the direction of each movement is used to reinforce the movement.

PERCEPTUAL-MOTOR PROGRAMS

Most of the perceptual-motor programs are carried on independently from the school and outside of the school situation. However, there are some schools that have acquired the services of a perceptual-motor specialist who operates within the framework

---

[6]Paul Smith, "Perceptual-Motor Skills and Readiness of Kindergarten Children," *Journal of Health, Physical Education and Recreation, vol. 41*, April 1970.

of the physical education program.

In general, perceptual-motor programs fall into the two broad categories of those that are considered to the *structured* and those that are considered to be *unstructured*. Since there are various degrees of structure in activities making up a given program, a considerable amount of overlapping can exist from one program to another. For example, there can be some degree of structure in a program that for all practical purposes would be classified as unstructured.

The structured program of perceptual-motor training is based on the notion that some form of structured physical activity can contribute to the development of a higher learning capacity in children with certain kinds of learning disabilities.[7] The unstructured type of program tends to be more creative in nature and is not so dependent upon a set of more or less "fixed" exercises. Play therapists have been aware of the value of the unstructured type of approach for years, as is shown by the following summary of a study by Bills some years ago.[8]

This study was an investigation of the effects of individual and group play on the reading level of retarded readers. As a result of the play therapy experiences it was concluded that (1) significant changes in reading ability occurred as a result of the play therapy experiences, and (2) personal changes may occur in nondirective play therapy in as little as six individual and three group play therapy sessions.

While a great deal of attention is currently being focused upon perceptual-motor programs, it should be made clear that such programs are not a panacea for all of the learning problems of children. However, if these types of programs (1) are geared to meet the individual needs of children, (2) remain within the realm of educational objectives, and (3) take into account the development of the child's *total* personality, they can become an important part of a multidisciplinary approach to some of the learning problems of children.

---

[7]S. Willard Footlik, "Perceptual-Motor Training and Cognitive Achievement: A Survey of the Literature," *Journal of Learning Disabilities,* January 1970.
[8]Robert E. Bills, "Nondirective Play Therapy with Retarded Readers," *Journal of Consulting Psychology, vol. 18* (1950).

Perhaps the point should be made again that compensatory physical education seeks to obtain much the same results as those obtained through organized perceptual-motor activities. The essential difference is that compensatory physical education tends to provide a way of improving learning ability which is free from uninteresting systematic activities. This is to say that the physical education experiences are likely to be more motivating and enjoyable.

EFFECT OF PERCEPTUAL-MOTOR TRAINING
ON ACADEMIC ACHIEVEMENT

A review of a large number of studies involving the effect of perceptual-motor programs and/or organized perceptual-motor activities on academic achievement revealed that about one-third of these were supportive or partially supportive of the procedure while the remaining two-thirds were nonsupportive. The following is a small sampling of these studies.

In attempting to determine the effect of perceptual-motor training on reading achievement in the first grade, Rosen[9] administered to twelve experimental classrooms a twenty-nine day adaptation of the Frostig Program for the development of visual perception, while thirteen control classrooms added comparable time to regular reading instruction. Pretesting and post-testing of experimental and control groups revealed that the former improved in visual perception but not in reading. The investigator felt that the additional time devoted to reading instruction might have been more important for reading achievement than the time devoted to perceptual training. The limitations of the study as seen by the investigator were the time and nature of the training program, the specific measuring instruments, and differential teacher effects. It was suggested by the investigator that it was quite possible that during the course of the school year control pupils, through normal growth, development and educational experiences that could not be controlled, acquired many perceptual skills that influenced their reading scores.

---

[9]Carl L. Rosen, "An Experimental Study of Visual Perceptual Training and Reading Achievement in the First Grade," *Perceptual and Motor Skills, vol. 22* (1966).

In a study using first grade children, one group received perceptual-motor training exclusively, another only regular physical education activities, and still another group no extra activities at all. The experiment was conducted for two 45-minute periods a week for seven weeks. The groups were tested for academic achievement at the beginning and at the end of the experiment. The results showed statistically significant gains for the group which received the perceptual-motor training but not for the other two groups. The investigators felt that they could not make any extensive generalizations on the basis of performance of such small groups in only one experiment. They recommended replication of the experiment on at least one other similar group in order to validate the results. They also suggested that they felt the perceptual-motor group might have improved more than the other groups because of the systematic training in focusing attention and in accurate listening that perceptual-motor training involves.[10]

A study conducted to determine whether children respond with higher scores on the Frostig test of visual perception after completion of the Frostig Visual-Perception Training Program utilized six schools with large proportions of disadvantaged children. In each of the six schools, six classes consisting of two prekindergarten, two kindergarten, and two first grade classes were selected. One class within each grade and each school was selected at random and received the Frostig Program, while other classes were identified as controls. In addition to the Frostig test, kindergarten experimental and control groups were given the Metropolitan Reading Readiness Test before and after the experiment. It was found that children showed greater gains on the Frostig test after having completed the Frostig Program than did the control pupils not receiving the program. However, the kindergarten experimental group which was given the reading readiness test did not show significantly greater gains than the control group in reading.[11]

---

[10]Clarence C. McCormick, et al., Improvement in Reading Achievement Through Perceptual-Motor Training," *Research Quarterly*, October 1968.
[11]James N. Jacobs, "An Evaluation of the Frostig Visual-Perceptual Training Program," *Educational Leadership*, January 1968.

A study was conducted to find if there was a relationship between performance scores in reading achievement, visual perception, motor development, two perceptual-motor tasks, and eye-hand dominance tests in seventy-five first grade and second grade children. Perceptual development level was evaluated by the Frostig Developmental Test of Visual Perception. Reading level was determined by the Metropolitan Achievement Test. The Lincoln-Oseretsky Motor Development Scale was used to evaluate the level of motor development. The two perceptual-motor tasks were designed by the investigator. Eye-hand dominance was determined by the pencil alignment test and the hole-in-card test. Appropriate statistical methods were used to determine the correlation between the variables and none were high enough for reliable prediction of one variable from another. Also no factors were in evidence that were indicative of interrelationships among the elements of visual, motor, and reading functions.[12]

In an attempt to test the value of providing special perceptual-motor training as part of the general kindergarten curriculum, sixty children designated as low on a school readiness test were randomly assigned to an experimental or control group. The groups were compared for readiness for reading at the end of the year and for reading achievement at the end of the second year. The results showed no significant differences and it was suggested that providing such special training as part of the general curriculum might be seriously questioned. Limitations of the study were: the difference in teaching ability, the number in the sample, the question as to the validity and reliability of the initial screening test, and the difficulty in scoring the tests.[13]

It is most important that the reader consider that the many research studies conducted in the area of perceptual-motor training do *not* present clear-cut and definitive evidence to support the notion that such programs result in academic achieve-

---

[12]Ella M. Trussell, "Relation of Performance of Selected Physical Skills to Perceptual Aspects of Reading Readiness in Elementary School Children," *Research Quarterly*, May 1968.

[13]Louis H. Falik, "The Effects of Special Perceptual-Motor Training in Kindergarten on Reading Readiness and on Second Reading Grade Performance," *Journal of Learning Disabilities*, August 1969.

ment. It should be recognized that many other variables can contribute to academic gains made by children. Certainly needing consideration are such factors as normal maturation, the influence of testing, systematic training in the focus of attention that perceptual-motor training involves, and the ever important aspect of teaching ability.

Chapter 3

USE OF BROAD CATEGORIES OF CURRICULUM CONTENT FOR COMPENSATORY PHYSICAL EDUCATION

THE broad categories of physical education curriculum content traditionally consist of *game activities, rhythmic activities,* and *self-testing activities.* Each of these categories is rich in possibilities for use in compensatory physical education. The purpose of this chapter is to consider generally each of these categories in terms of their value for compensatory physical education. In succeeding chapters, specific activities from the three broad categories will be presented with respect to certain factors inherent in the activities which may be useful in improving learning ability.

GAME ACTIVITIES

For our purposes here, we will consider games as *active interactions of children in competitive and/or cooperative situations.* This description of games places emphasis on active games as opposed to those that are passive in nature. This is to say that games in physical education are concerned with the total, or near total, physical response of children as they interact with each other.

Competition and Cooperation in Games

It should be emphasized that the above description of games takes into account both competitive and cooperative situations. In view of the fact that there has been a considerable amount of interest in competitive activities for children of elementary school age, it seems appropriate that we discuss this because games play a large part in compensatory physical education.

It is interesting to note that the terms *cooperation* and *competition* are antonymous; therefore, the reconciliation of children's competitive needs and cooperative needs is not an easy matter. In a sense we are confronted with an ambivalent condition which, if not carefully handled, could place children in a state of conflict. Horney recognized this many years ago when she indicated that on the one hand everything is done to spur us toward success, which means that we must not only be assertive but aggressive, able to push others out of the way. On the other hand, we are deeply imbued with ideals which influence us to think it selfish to want anything for ourselves, that we should be humble, turn the other cheek, be yielding.[1] Thus, modern society not only rewards one kind of behavior (cooperation) but its direct opposite (competition). Perhaps more often than not our cultural demands sanction these rewards without clear-cut value standards regarding specific conditions under which these forms of behavior may be practiced. Hence, the child is placed in somewhat of a quandary; when does he compete and when does he cooperate?

In generalizing on the basis of the available evidence with regard to the subject of competition, it seems justifiable to formulate the following concepts:

1. Very young children in general are not very competitive but become more so as they grow older.
2. There is a wide variety of competition among children; that is, some are violently competitive, while others are mildly competitive, and still others are not competitive at all.
3. Boys tend to be more competitive than girls.
4. Competition should be adjusted so that there is not a preponderance of winners over losers.
5. Competition and rivalry produce results in effort and speed of accomplishment.

In compensatory physical education teaching-learning situations teachers might well be guided by the above concepts. As far as active games are concerned, they are not only a good medium for improving learning ability through compensatory physical

---

[1]Karen Horney, *The Neurotic Personality of Our Times* (New York: W. W. Norton and Company, Inc.): 1937.

education but, under the guidance of skillful teachers, they can also provide for competitive needs of children in a pleasurable and enjoyable way.

Some Thoughts on the Use of Games for Compensatory Physical Education

The value of games as an important intellectual influence in the school program has been recognized for decades. For example, as far back as 1909, Bancroft observed that a child's perceptions are quickened, he sees more quickly that the ball is coming toward him, that he is in danger of being tagged, or that it is his turn; he hears footsteps behind him, or his name or number called; he feels the touch on the shoulder; or in innumerable other ways he is aroused to quick and direct recognition of, and response to, things that go on around him.[2]

In recent years there has been concern among some sociologists and psychologists about what they feel has been a decline in the use of games in the lives of children. This they attribute in part to changes in the life-style and culture of certain segments of American society. Some psychologists have noted that this decline has been notable from the late 1950s to the early 1970s. It is speculated that during this time many of the perceptual-motor programs have become well known and that remedial techniques used in these programs are an attempt to fill the gap left by the loss of games in which children once participated. In addition, it has been pointed out that these techniques cannot fully take the place of children's games any more than toys can take the place of mother's pots and pans and the contents of the food cupboards. And, further, that whereas the remedial techniques attempt to forge a link between one or two of the sense modalities, the games of children not only link up the sense modalities but also add to the child's feelings of competence in relationship to peers and to his feelings of self-worth in relationship to handling well the rules of the game — feelings that remedial techniques cannot generate, as they are aimed at remedying a deficit the child is quite

---

[2]Jessie H. Bancroft, *Games* (New York: The MacMillan Company): 1909.

aware of possessing. Moreover, the playing of a game is integrated with a general feeling of activity, whereas remedial techniques are inextricably linked with a generalized feeling of passivity in the child.[3]

It is most unfortunate that in about the same time frame mentioned above some individuals in physical education were recommending the abandonment of games in early childhood. This could have been due in part to the "bandwagon syndrome" that accompanied the introduction of the *movement education* approach adopted from Great Britain. That is, some persons spent so much time with this approach that active games were curtailed to a large extent. Nevertheless, it is encouraging to find that games are being recommended again by many educators as an important and worthwhile part of the regular school program.[4]

Illustration of the Use of Games in Compensatory Physical Education

An example of how certain games can help children with learning difficulties is seen in the positive responses to the games by children with slow reaction time. This is the amount of time that it takes a person to get an overt response started after receiving a stimulus, or, more simply, the stimulus to response interval. Such children ordinarily have difficulty in processing input from an auditory and/or visual stimulus. When this occurs some teachers may tend to feel that the child is not interested and lacks enthusiasm. This condition can be improved over a period of time by games requiring auditory and/or visual input as a starting signal. One such game is *Crows and Cranes* which involves auditory input. The game is played in the following manner.

The playing area is divided by a center line. The group is divided into two teams. The children of one team are designated as Crows and take positions on one side of the area, with the base

---

[3]Sophie L. Lovinger, "Learning Disabilities and Games," *Academic Therapy*, vol. IX, no. 3 (Winter 1973-74).
[4]Loyda M. Shears and Eli M. Bower, *Games in Education and Development* (Springfield, Illinois, Charles C Thomas Publisher, 1974).

line on their side serving as their safety zone. The members of the other team are designated as Cranes and take positions on the other side of the area, with their base line as a safety zone. The teams are three or four feet apart. The teacher stands to one side of the area by the center line, and then calls out either "Crows" or "Cranes." If the teacher calls the Crows, they turn and run to their base line to avoid being tagged. The Cranes attempt to tag their opponents before they cross their baseline. The Cranes score a point for each Crow tagged. The Crows and Cranes then return to their places, and the teacher calls one or the other groups; play continues in the same manner. As the teacher observes certain children reacting slowly they can be grouped together.

The game of *Black and White* is played in the same manner but uses visual input. One team is the "Blacks," and the other the "Whites." An object, black on one side and white on the other, is tossed into the air. If it comes down on the black side, the Blacks run for their base line, and vice versa. All procedures are the same as for Crows and Cranes except that the children react to visual input rather than auditory input.

The following simulated teaching-learning situation using the game *Crows and Cranes* indicates how this activity can be employed to help children sort out auditory stimuli, thus improving listening skills.

TEACHER: Children, today we are going to learn a new game, but first I want to see how well you can listen, because you must listen closely for the game we are going to play. Now listen closely. I am going to say two sentences and I am going to leave one word out of each sentence. I will tell you the sound with which that word begins. You are to use that sound and the meaning of the other words to decide what word I leave out. Does everyone understand? Fine, let's begin. The word I am going to leave out of the first sentence begins with the same sound as cream, crow, cranes. Now listen. The little boy was so unhappy that he began to (*pause*). What word did I leave out?
PUPIL: I know. The boy began to cry.
TEACHER: That's right the word was cry. Now let's try the second one. Children like to eat ice (*pause*) cones. What was the word that time?

PUPIL: That's easy! Cream.

TEACHER: Fine. Now the new game we are going to play is one in which we will use the new sound that we have learned. The name of the game is Crows and Cranes and the new sound is "cr." Get into the same groups we were in the other day for Hill Dill. Bring your lines close together. This side will be the Crows and this side will be the Cranes. We will use the same goals that we used for Hill Dill. I will call out either Crows or Cranes. If I call Crows, all the Crows will turn and run to the goal and the Cranes will try to tag as many as they can. If I call Cranes, the Crows will chase the Cranes in the same way. Now we will have to listen closely for the new sound. Are you ready?

(Pupils participate in the game for a specified amount of time and then the teacher evaluates the activity with them.)

TEACHER: You seemed to have fun playing Crows and Cranes. What were some of the things you liked about it?

PUPIL: I like to run.

PUPIL: I like to chase and tag.

PUPIL: I caught two at once.

TEACHER: Yes, there were many things that you liked about it. What do we have to do in order to be good at this game?

PUPIL: Well, for one thing, you have to be able to run fast.

PUPIL: You have to listen so you know when to run.

TEACHER: If we played it again, can you think of any ways to make it a better game? Should we always use the words "Crows and Cranes?"

PUPIL: We could change the words.

TEACHER: How do you mean, George?

PUPIL: Maybe we could use other words that begin with the same two letters. Say, like "gray and green."

TEACHER: I think that is a splendid idea. We will try the game again tomorrow and I would like to have you think of as many words as you can that we might use in this game.

RHYTHMIC ACTIVITIES

For purposes of the discussion here, rhythmic activities are described as those human movement experiences that *require* some sort of rhythmical accompaniment. Some authorities consider the meaning of the term "dance" to be broader than the term "rhythmic activities." However, the point of view here is that there are certain human movement experiences that require some form of rhythmical accompaniment that do not necessarily have the same objectives as those ordinarily associated with dance.

The term "rhythm" is derived from the Greek word *rhythmos,* which means "measured motion." One need only to look at the functions of the human body to see the importance of rhythm in the life of the elementary school child. The heart beats in rhythm, the digestive processes function in rhythm, breathing is done in rhythm; in fact, almost anything in which human beings are involved is done in a more or less rhythmic pattern.

There are many ways of classifying rhythmic activities. One approach centers around the kind of *rhythmic experiences* that one might wish children to have. It is recommended here that as an aspect of compensatory physical education rhythmic experiences might consist of (1) unstructured experiences, (2) semistructured experiences, and (3) structured experiences. It should be understood that in this particular way of grouping rhythmic experiences a certain amount of overlapping will occur as far as the degree of structuring is concerned. That is, although an experience is classified as an unstructured one, there could possibly be some small degree of structuring in certain kinds of situations. With this idea in mind the following descriptions of these three kinds of rhythmic experiences are submitted.

Unstructured experiences include those in which there is an original or creative response and in which there has been little, if any, previous explanation or discussion in the form of specific directions. The *semistructured* experiences include those in which certain movements are suggested by the teacher, a child, or group of children. *Structured* experiences involve the more difficult rhythmic patterns associated with the various types of dances.

The various forms of rhythmic experiences have been used with success with learning disability children. Painter found that a program of systematic rhythmic and sensorimotor activities resulted in significant gains in body image, perceptual-motor integration, and psycholinguistic competence in low-functioning kindergarten children.[5] In reporting about neurological dysfunctioning in the visual-perceptual-auditory motor areas, William McClurg implied that disabled readers frequently lack coordination in such basic motor movements as walking and running. And further, that motor *rhythm* is often lacking in persons with reading, writing, and spelling problems.[6]

As mentioned in the previous chapter, a condition often related to dominance as far as reading is concerned is that of *reversals.* One type of reversal (static) refers to a child seeing letters reversed such as *n* and *b* appearing as *u* and *d.* In another type (kinetic) the child may see the word *no* as *on.* In some instances it has been found that children with the kinetic type of reversal also have a condition known as "arhythmia" (lack of rhythm). Attempts have been made to provide certain kinds of rhythmic movements for such children in order to correct this condition. It is possible that this approach may have much to commend it and varying degrees of success have been attained with it. It is interesting to note that in this general connection Drake found that by working with dyslexic children in fine motor skills such as handwriting, and patterned motor skills — especially folk dancing — improvement in reading was in evidence.[7]

A very important type of rhythmic activity for children with learning disabilities is creative rhythms (unstructured experience), where the child responds by expressing himself in a way that the rhythmical accompaniment makes him feel. When a child is able to use his body freely there is a strong likelihood that there will be increased body awareness. Creative rhythms will also give the child free self-direction in space, as well as self-control, in that he is not involved with a partner in a more formalized rhythmic activity. It has been found that creative rhythms provide a situation for children with learning disabilities where they

---

[5]Genevieve Painter, "The effect of a rhythmic and sensory motor activity program on perceptual-motor spatial ability of kindergarten children," *Exceptional Children, 33* (1969): p. 113.

[6]William H. McClurg, "The neurophysiological basis of reading disabilities," *The Reading Teacher,* April 1969.

[7]Charles Drake, "Reading, 'Riting, and Rhythm," *The Reading Teacher,* December 1964.

cannot fail. There are no rules to remember, no criteria for "good" or "bad." All he is asked to do is contribute his own ideas.[8]

While great emphasis has been placed upon creative rhythms for the child with a learning disability, this should in no way minimize the value and importance of performing activities such as dancing, which are within the framework of an established pattern (structured experience). This is particularly true as far as emotional release is concerned. Mental hygienists know that some persons can express themselves with more spontaneity in a relatively structured situation than in one where they have more freedom (possibly a factor in the work by Drake reported above). Such persons, when they skip, dance, clap and twirl to the rhythm of the music may be expressing themselves with an abandon that is not possible when they are free to express themselves in any way they wish.[9]

In addition, many forms of structured dance patterns contain various inherent perceptual-motor developmental factors as follows:

1. For children who have difficulty with sequencing (following a sequence of activities) dancing affords an opportunity to follow simple steps or procedures which can lead to the more complex patterns.
2. Dancing involves left and right directionality, and at times may involve constant changing of directions.
3. The identification and use of certain parts of the body such as arms, hands, feet and legs are essential in some dances. Being called upon to use parts of the body may help establish one's image of body and body parts.
4. In such rhythmic activities as singing games where accompaniment is furnished through song, it is the auditory clues that guide the movement. Thus, an opportunity is provided for practice in auditory discrimination.

SELF-TESTING ACTIVITIES

Those physical education activities based upon the child's

---

[8]Toni Carter, "Creative dramatics for LD Children," *Academic Therapy*, vol. IX, no. 6 (Summer 1974): p. 413.

[9]Emma M. Layman, in *Science and Medicine of Exercise and Sports*, 2nd ed., eds, W. R. Johnson and E. R. Buskirk (New York, Harper and Row Publishers, 1974).

desire to test his ability in such a way that he attempts to better his performance may be placed in the broad category of self-testing activities. For the most part these activities involve competing against oneself and natural forces. Among others, such activities as stunts and tumbling, exercises with or without apparatus and individual skill proficiency in locomotor skills, and skills of propulsion and retrieval can be classified in this broad category.

One of the major values ordinarily attributed to self-testing activities is their specific contribution to such elements of physical fitness as strength, agility, coordination, and flexibility. Zealous proponents of self-testing activities stoutly maintain that contributions to these various factors are more likely to accrue through self-testing activities than may be the case through games and rhythmic activities. The reason for this lies in the fact that successful performance of certain self-testing activities requires the involvement of the various elements of physical fitness. An opportunity to participate and practice individually in self-testing activities is provided for the children with learning disabilities.

It has also been suggested by many teachers that some of these activities help to build courage, confidence, and poise in children, although this is difficult to evaluate objectively. Following are some representative examples of classifications of self-testing activities in which various aspects of perceptual-motor development are inherent.

Stunts and Tumbling

Certain stunt and tumbling activities can be of value in providing for perceptual-motor development. For example, since reading is a perceptual skill involving bilateral movement, certain stunts involving such movements might be used to advantage. It has also been found that certain stunts are useful in helping to improve body awareness. Stunts which alert the child to the movement of certain muscle groups when he presses against something can be of value for this purpose. Such a stunt is the *Chinese Get Up*. This activity involves two pupils. These two pupils sit with their backs to each other and with their feet close to their buttocks. They lock arms at their elbows and keep them bent close to their sides. The two pupils then lean back against each other and straighten their legs until they are both in a standing position. They may need to use short walking steps to get to the standing position.

In tumbling activities involving some of the simple rolls there is an opportunity to use those parts of the body, for example the torso, less sensitive to *tactile* perception than other parts of the body. In this regard it has been suggested by Smith[10] that through such tumbling activities as the *Log Roll* the child is given the opportunity to explore the environment *tactilely* with the body and its segments. The Log Roll is performed by having the pupil assume an extended prone position with his stomach facing toward the mat. The extended body position along the vertical axis is accomplished by placing the arms over the head along the mat until they are straight. The legs are also extended with the feet together and the toes pointed. The pupil then uses his head, shoulders and hips to turn 360 degrees along the mat. The pupil should learn to roll in both directions and in a straight line down the mat.

Trampoline

Although the trampoline is not used on a widespread basis, under careful and skilled supervision and guidance it can be very useful in developing better awareness of self and concepts of spatial realtionships. Kephart,[11] one of the early exponents of the value of the trampoline in perceptual-motor training, suggested that not only must the child learn a dynamic relationship to the center of gravity and maintain a dynamic balance, but he must maintain these coordinations under changing relationships. In addition, the changes in these relationships are not the result of his own effort directly, but are dependent in a large part on the

---

[10]Hope M. Smith, "Implications for movement education experiences drawn from perceptual-motor research," *Journal of Health, Physical Education and Recreation*, April 1970.

[11]Newell C. Kephart, *The Slow Learner in the Classroom* (Columbus, Ohio, Charles E. Merrill Books, 1960).

trampoline and its functions. Thus, the timing and rhythm of his activity are dictated by the spring of the trampoline rather than directly determined by his own movements. In activities on the surface area the child can adjust his movements to the rhythm pattern of his muscles. Thus, if the neurological innervation to one or more muscle groups loses its rhythm, he merely adjusts his movements to this change. On the trampoline, such adjustment is not possible, since the rhythm is dictated by the device. Therefore, he must learn to maintain adequate and constant rhythms in his neuromuscular coordination which are demanded in few other activities. Thus, the mere activity of bouncing on the trampoline contributes to body image and the awareness of spatial relationships within the body.

Some research has been conducted in connection with the benefits to be derived from the use of the trampoline as a perceptual-motor medium. An example is the work of McCants.[12] In a controlled study to determine the effects of an eight-week instructional program of trampolining upon selected measures of physical fitness of mentally retarded and emotionally disturbed children in a special school it was found that the experimental group improved significantly on all tests. It was also observed that there were other improvements in the experimental group in the way of classroom performance, social adjustment, morale, and confidence. An interesting aside to this study was that the investigator was employed immediately to continue the program for the rest of the children in the school.

Balance Beam

Activities on the balance beam can help the child maintain his relationship to gravity, and at the same time help to develop space awareness and directionally related movements.

Attempts to study the relationship between reading and ability to perform dynamic balance have yielded varying results. In one

---

[12]Robert McCants, "Effects of an eight week trampoline instruction program on certain measures of the physical fitness of retarded children," Masters Thesis, University of Maryland, College Park, Maryland, 1962.

such study, Walker [13] compared balance beam walking test scores with reading readiness test scores of 162 first grade children. On the basis of his data he generalized that (1) there seemed to be a tendency for first grade children scoring high or low on the reading readiness test to score respectively high or low on the balance beam walking test; (2) there seemed to be a much greater relationship between balance beam walking test scores and reading readiness test scores of girls than boys; and (3) girls tended to score higher than boys on the balance beam walking test. It is important to recognize that these are not cause and effect relationships but co-existent behaviors.

Ball Handling Activities

Such skills with inflated balls as tapping (bouncing), throwing to a partner or target, and catching can often be useful in helping children develop eye-hand coordination, timing, and bilaterality.

Ordinarily, children with eye-hand coordination problems have difficulty catching a ball, not necessarily because of a motor response but more likely, perhaps, because of slowness in eye movement. It may be a good practice with some children to simply roll the ball slowly across the surface area and have them follow it with their eyes. Several children can sit in a circle and roll the ball back and forth to each other. Later they can work on catching a ball at a short distance in the air. A beach ball or even a balloon may be good to begin with because the lighter weight of this type of object will cause it to move more slowly through the air. Under the condition of easily being able to follow the object visually, the child should be more successful in catching it. (This pertains to short distances only.)

Bouncing a ball can be used advantageously to improve timing. Sometimes it is helpful to accompany bouncing with some sort of rhythm. In their first experience with ball bouncing, many children tend to "slap" the ball hard, causing it to rebound in a way that is difficult to control. One way to help avoid this is to suggest

---

[13]James Walker, A Comparison of Lee-Clark Reading Readiness Scores with a test of balance using selected first grade children. Master's Thesis, University of Maryland, College Park, Maryland, 1963.

that the ball is a friend and should be treated as such ("as you might pat your puppy dog").

In this chapter we have dealt generally with broad categories. In succeeding chapters specific activities for particular perceptual-motor deficiencies will be presented. However, it must be borne in mind that specific classification of the various perceptual-motor areas is practically impossible. This is due to the fact that there is so much overlapping from one area to another, that no one area is a separate entity unto itself. For example, laterality and directionality are of vital importance in body image, and all are concerned with visual perception. Obviously, this interrelationship of all of the areas has made it difficult to place physical education activities neatly into specific areas as far as their contribution to a given perceptual-motor deficiency is concerned. This is to say that some of the activities in the following chapters could be placed in more than one classification with satisfactory results.

Chapter 4

BODY-CONCEPT

IN order to put the idea of body-concept in its proper perspective, consideration needs to be given to the more basic aspects of *self-structure* and *self-concept*. According to Perkins,[1] self-structure is the framework of a particular individual's complex of motives, perceptions, cognitions, feelings, and values — the product of developmental processes. Self-structure is revealed in behavior. One reveals in his behavior the knowledge, skills, and interests he has acquired, the goals he is seeking, the beliefs, values, and attitudes he has adopted, the roles he has learned, and the self-concept he has formed. Thus, self-concept is an aspect of self-structure.

It is also suggested by Perkins that among the most relevant and significant perceptions that an individual acquires are those of himself in various life situations. And further, that basically, the self-concept is made up of a large number of *percepts*, each of which contains one or more qualities that one ascribes to himself. To be more specific, *self-percept* pertains to sense impressions of a trait one ascribes to himself, while *self-concept* consists of the totality of one's self-percepts organized in some sort of order.

The frames of reference with which we are concerned here are the physical processes and the self-concept. This is to say that our primary interest focuses upon the physical self or *body-concept*, the physical aspect of the total personality. One point of departure in discussing the physical aspect of personality could be to say that "everybody has a body." Some are short, some are tall, some are lean, and some are fat. Children come in different sizes but all of them have a certain innate physical capacity which is influenced by the environment.

It might be said of the child that he *is* his body. It is something he can see. It is his base of operation — what we might well

---

[1]Hugh Perkins, *Human Development and Learning*, 2nd ed. (Belmont, California, Wadsworth Publishing Company, 1974): p. 247.

identify as the "physical base." The other components of the total personality — social, emotional and intellectual — are somewhat vague as far as the child is concerned. Although these are manifested in various ways, the child does not actually see them as he does the physical aspect. Consequently, it becomes all-important that the child be helped early in life to gain control over the physical aspect, or what is known as basic body control, and to develop a positive body-concept. The implementation of this through physical education activities is the function of this chapter.

THE PROBLEM OF TERMINOLOGY

Communication in this particular area is complicated by a lack of standardization in the use of certain terms. For example, Brooke and Whiting[2] point this up very clearly when they state that "problems of terminology make this a difficult field for evaluation .... The following terms, for example, have been utilized by different writers for the same or related concepts: body-schema, body-image, body-awareness, body-concept, body-sense, and body-experience."

The *Dictionary of Education*[3] describes the broad term *self-image* as "the perceptual component of self; the image one has of the appearance of his body; the picture one has of the impression he makes on others." This same source defines the more specific term *body-image* as "a conceptual construct of one's own body as it relates to orientation, body movement and other types of behavior."

The essential difference in these two definitions is that self-image has to do with the appearance of the body, while body-image is more concerned with how the individual conceives his own body in terms of its interaction with the environment.

In differentiating between the terms *body-image* and *body-awareness* Whiting et. al.[4] consider body-image as "an image of

[2]J. D. Brooke and H. T. A. Whiting, *Human Movement: A Field of Study* (London, Henry Kimpton Publishers, 1973).
[3]Carter V. Good, *Dictionary of Education,* 2nd ed. (New York, McGraw-Hill Book Company, 1959): p. 279.
[4]H. T. A. Whiting et al., *Personality and Performance in Physical Education and Sport,* (London, Henry Kimpton Publishers, 1973).

his own body which the individual has evolved through experience" and *body-awareness* "an appreciation and understanding of the body as the instrument of movement and vehicle of expression in nonverbal communication."

It is interesting to note that Morris and Whiting[5] observe that the term *body-awareness* has widespread use among physical educators. This has been my experience since an extensive review of the physical education literature on this general subject has revealed that the term "body-awareness" is used much more frequently than other terms. Throughout this chapter it is possible that some of the different terms will be used to convey the same meaning.

DETERMINING PROBLEMS OF BODY-AWARENESS

It is doubtful that there are any absolutely foolproof methods of detecting problems of body-awareness in children. The reason for this is that many mannerisms said to be indicative of body-awareness problems can also be symptomatic of other deficiencies. Nevertheless, those persons who are likely to deal in some way with children in compensatory physical education should be alert to detect certain possible deficiencies.

Generally speaking, there are two ways in which deficiencies concerned with body-awareness might be detected. First, some deficiencies can be discerned, at least in part, by observing certain behaviors. And, second, there are some relatively simple diagnostic techniques which can be used to detect such deficiencies. The following generalized list contains examples of both of these possibilities and is submitted to assist the reader in this particular regard.

1. One technique often used to diagnose possible problems of body-awareness is to have children make a drawing of themselves. The primary purpose of this is to see if certain parts of the body are not included in the drawing. My own personal experience several years ago as a Certified Binet Intelligence

---

[5]P. R. Morris, and H. T. A. Whiting, *Motor Impairment and Compensatory Education* (Philadelphia, Lea & Fegiber, 1971).

Test Examiner revealed possibilities for such a diagnosis inherent in the test item involving *picture completion*. In this test item a partial drawing of a "man" is provided for the child to complete. Since the child's interest in drawing a man dates from his earliest attempts to represent things symbolically, it is possible, through typical drawings by young children, to trace certain characteristic stages of perceptual development. It has also been found in recent years that the procedure of drawing a picture of himself assists in helping to detect if there is lack of body-awareness. (One of my own experiments concerning this phenomenon is presented later in the chapter.)

2. Sometimes the child with a lack of body-awareness may manifest tenseness in his movements. At the same time he may be unsure of his movements as he attempts to move the body segments.

3. Some persons tend to feel that a child with a reversal problem may also have problems with body-awareness. (The reader should refer back to the previous chapter with regard to reversals and rhythmic activities.)

4. If the child is instructed to move a body part such as placing one foot forward, he may direct his attention to the body part before making the movement. Or, he may look at another child to observe the movement before he attempts to make the movement himself. This could be due to poor processing of the input (auditory or visual stimulus) provided for the movement.

5. When instructed to use one body part (arm) he may also move the corresponding body part (other arm) when it is not necessary. For example, he may be asked to swing the right arm and he may also start to swing the left arm simultaneously.

6. In such activities as catching an object, the child may turn toward the object when this is not necessary. For example, when a beanbag thrown to him approaches close to the child, he may move forward with either side of the body rather than trying to retrieve the beanbag with his hands while both feet remain stationary.

ACTIVITIES INVOLVING BODY-AWARENESS

In general, it might be said that when a child is given the opportunity to use his body freely in enjoyable movement an increase in body-awareness occurs. More specifically, there are activities which can be useful in helping children identify and understand the use of various body parts as well as the relationship of these parts.

Over a period of years I have conduced a number of experiments in an attempt to determine the effect of participation in certain physical education activities on body-awareness. The following is an example of this quasi-objective approach utilizing the game *Busy Bee*.

In this game the children are in pairs facing each other and dispersed around the activity area. One child who is the *caller* is in the center of the area. He makes calls such as "shoulder-to-shoulder," "toe-to-toe," or "hand-to-hand." (In the early stages of the game it might be a good idea to have the teacher do the calling.) As the calls are made, the paired children go through the appropriate motions with their partners. After a few calls, the caller will shout, "Busy Bee!" This is the signal for every child to get a new partner, including the caller. The child who does not get a partner can become the new caller.

This game has been experimented with in the following manner: As the children played the game, the teacher made them aware of the location of various parts of the body in order to develop the concept of full body-image.

Before the game was played, the children were asked to draw a picture of themselves. Many did not know how to begin, and others omitted some of the major limbs in their drawings. After playing Busy Bee, the children were asked again to draw a picture of themselves. This time they were more successful. All of the drawings had bodies, heads, arms, and legs. Some of them had hands, feet, eyes, and ears. A few even had teeth and hair.

Some activities are concerned with the process of identification in terms of certain characteristics that children might possess. The following simulated teaching-learning situation shows how a teacher might originally introduce the concept of body-awareness using the game *Have You Seen My Sheep?*

The players may stand or be seated in a circle. One player is selected to be *It* to act as a "farmer" or a "shepherd." He walks around the outside of the circle, stops behind one of the pupils, and asks, "Have you seen my sheep?" The pupil responds by asking, "What does your sheep look like?" *It* then describes another player in the circle while the second pupil tries to determine who is being described. As soon as he finds out from the description who the described player is, he chases that individual around the outside of the circle, trying to tag him before he can run around the circle and return to his place. If the player is tagged, he becomes *It*. If he is not tagged, the chaser is *It* and the game is repeated. The original *It* does not take part in this chase, but steps into the circle in the space vacated by the chaser. If the game is played in the classroom, the pupils may sit in their seats. The person described runs for safety to a designated empty seat. The person who was *It* goes back to his own seat.

TEACHER: In reading we have learned that some words look alike, and some have small differences. Each boy and girl looks like some other one in one way or another, but each has an individual look that makes him or her different from anyone else. Do you think you would recognize yourself if I described you?

PUPIL: If you said a boy with red hair, I would know who it is.

TEACHER: That would be easy because Frank is the only boy with red hair in our class. Do you think you could describe someone else so that we could recognize him or her?

PUPIL: Can I try it first?

TEACHER: We can play a game where we can see if we can describe others and also recognize ourselves when we are described. The game is called "Have You Seen My Sheep?" Will you make a circle? Fred, let's make believe you are a farmer and that you have lost one of your sheep. You will walk around the circle and tap someone on the back. Then you will say to that person, "Have you seen my sheep?" The person that you tap will ask, "What does your sheep look like?" You will then tell the person what your sheep looks like, describing one of the children in the circle. When the one you tapped guesses the person in the circle you are describing, he chases him around the circle and tries to tag him before he can return to his place. Does everyone understand how to play the game?

PUPIL: What happens if you get caught?

PUPIL: Is the sheep *It?*

TEACHER: Yes, the sheep then becomes the farmer and the game is played again.

(The children play the game and the teacher evaluates it with them)

TEACHER: George, you seemed to be having a good time. What did you like about that game?

PUPIL: I like to be chased, and I didn't get caught.

TEACHER: How can we help each other in this game?

PUPIL: We have to listen when someone is talking.

TEACHER: We learned how to play a new game that was fun. What else did we learn?

PUPIL: We learned that some of us look alike in some ways.

PUPIL: And we learned that we are different in some ways.

PUPIL: We used color words and we used the names of kinds of clothes that kids wear.

TEACHER: How were you able to tell who the sheep was?

PUPIL: By listening to the person tell about him.

TEACHER: What did those of you who were farmers find that you had to do in telling about the sheep? What do you think, Jane?

PUPIL: I had to be able to tell Mary exactly what George looked like. I had to explain it to her so she could tell who I was talking about.

TEACHER: Fine! You seemed to have fun and also you saw the need for being able to explain something to someone else.

The following activities have been divided into the three broad categories of physical education content described in the previous chapter, that is, *game* activities, *rhythmic* activities, and *self-testing* activities. The reader should note that among the activities will be found those which can be used for diagnosis, body-awareness improvement, evaluation of body-awareness status or various combinations of these factors. Some of the activities are age-old while others have been developed for specific conditions.

Some of the activities are in the form of stories which I have developed for the purpose of using physical education experiences to improve upon listening and reading. Each of the activities contains a description of how it is performed along with a comment detailing certain other aspects of the activity.

Game Activities

Everybody Goes

All of the children (except the one who is *It*) line up side by side at one end of the activity area. *It* stands in the middle of the activity area facing the line. At the opposite end of the area there is a goal line. The distance of the playing area can be variable. The game is started with the following rhyme:

Head, shoulders, knees, and toes.
Eyes, ears, mouth, and nose.
Off and running everybody goes.

On the last word, "goes," the children in the line run to the other end and try to reach the goal line without being tagged by *It*. All of those tagged become helpers for *It* and the game continues with the children running to the opposite end on the signal. If the game is played in its entirety it continues until there is one player left who can be declared the winner.

As the rhyme is recited, the children in the line do the following motions: Head — place both hands on the head, shoulders — place both hands on the shoulders; knees — bend at the waist and place hands on the knees; toes — bend on down and touch the toes and resume standing position; eyes — point to the eyes; ears — point to the ears; mouth — point to the mouth; nose — point to the nose.

Comment: It might be a good idea in the early stages for the teacher to recite the rhyme. The teacher can be the judge of how fast this should be done. The more accomplished the children become, the faster the rhyme can be recited, and the children themselves can recite it in unison. When the game is first played, the teacher can observe closely for those children who are reacting by doing what the rhyme says. It may be found that some are having difficulty. Thus, the activity becomes a means for diagnosing a lack of body-awareness. It will be noted that with practice children will improve in their response to the rhyme. A different form of locomotion can be submitted for *running*. That is, it can be "Off and skipping (hopping, jumping, etc.) everybody goes."

Come With Me

Several children form a circle with one child outside the circle. The child outside the circle walks around it, taps another child and says, "Come with me." The child tapped falls in behind the first child and they continue walking around the circle. The second child taps a child and says, "Come with me." This continues until several children have been tapped. At a given point the first child calls out, "Go home!" On this signal all the children try to get back to their original place in the circle. The first child also tries to get into one of these places. There will be one child left out. He can be the first child for the next game.

Comment: In the early stages of this game the teacher should call out where each child is to be tapped. For example, "on the arm," "on the leg, etc." After a while the child doing the tapping can call out where he is going to tap the child. The teacher can observe if children are tapped in the proper place.

Mirrors

One child is selected as the leader and stands in front of a line of children. This child goes through a variety of different movements and the children in the line try to do exactly the same thing, that is they act as mirrors. The leader should be changed frequently.

Comment: In this activity the children become aware of different body parts and movements as the child in front makes the various movements. The teacher should be alert to see how well and how quickly the children are able to do the movements that the leader makes.

Move Along

The children lie on their backs on the floor. The teacher gives a signal such as the beat of a drum or clap of the hands and the children move their arms and legs in any way they choose. The teacher then gives the name of a movement such as "Move your legs like a bicycle," and then gives the signal to begin the movement. If the teacher wishes, some sort of scoring system can be devised to reward those children who make the correct movement in the fastest amount of time.

Comment: The teacher should observe closely to see how rapidly the children respond to the movements called. In addition, the teacher should observe to see if some children are waiting to see what others are going to do before making the correct movement.

Change Circles

Several circles are drawn on the floor or outdoor activity area with one less circle than the number of participants. The one child who does not have a circle can be *It* and stands in the middle of the area. The teacher calls out signals in the form of body parts. For example, such calls would include, "hands on knees," "hands on head," "right hand on your left foot," and so on. After a time the teacher calls out, "Change circles!" whereupon all the children try to get into a different circle while the child who is *It* tries to find a circle. The child who does not find a circle can be *It* or a new person can be chosen to be *It*.

Comment: The teacher should observe closely to see how the children react to the calls, and whether or not they are looking at the other children for clues. As time goes on and the children become more familiar with body parts, more complicated calls can be made.

Simon Says

The children stand about the activity area facing the person who plays Simon. Every time Simon says to do something, the children must do it. However, if a command is given without the prefix *Simon Says*, the children remain motionless. For example, when the leader issues the command "Simon says, put your hands on your knees," everyone is to place his hands on his knees. But if the person playing Simon says, "Lift your left foot," no one should move. If desired, some sort of scoring method can be used for following the commands correctly.

Comment: Perhaps in the early stages it might be a good idea for the teacher to control the activity by taking the part of Simon. Later, different children can be selected for this role. The teacher can observe whether or not children are reacting correctly. After the children become accustomed to the game, the commands can become more difficult and can be given at a more rapid rate.

Draw a Picture Relay

Several columns of children with an equal number in each are formed and face the chalkboard. The object of this relay is to have each team draw a picture of a man on the chalkboard. The first child in each column runs to the chalkboard and draws a part. The next child adds to this part and this continues until all have had an opportunity to contribute to the drawing. The winner is declared on the basis of which team finishes first along with the one which had the best drawing. The children decide which drawing was the best.

Comment: This can become a very hilarious activity since all sorts of funny pictures can result from it. It may be that the drawing was not completed because there were not enough children to make the complete drawing. This can then be used as a discussion as to which parts were missing. In their haste children will often place parts in the wrong place. This can also be used for discussion as to where is the proper place for a particular body part or segment.

Body Tag

In this game one child is selected to be *It*. He chases the other children and attempts to tag one of them. If he is successful the child tagged can become *It*. If *It* does not succeed within a reasonable amount of time a new *It* should be selected. In order to be officially tagged, a specific part of the body must be tagged by *It*. Thus, the game could be shoulder tag, arm tag, or leg tag as desired.

Comment: The teacher observes the child to see whether or not he tags the correct body part. To add more interest to the activity, the teacher can call out the part of the body to be tagged during each session of the game.

Birds Fly South

All of the children except one who is *It* assemble at the end of the activity area. At the other end of the activity area a goal line is designated. *It* calls out "Birds fly south with hands on knees," or the hands touching any other part of the body. The children take this position as does *It*. They try to run to the opposite end and try to avoid being tagged by *It*. All of those tagged become helpers for *It*; if the game continues in its entirety all but one player would be tagged. This player can be *It* for next time or a new *It* can be selected.

Comment: The teacher observes whether or not the children assume the correct position before starting to run. If so desired *It* can call out only the words "Birds fly south" and the teacher can add the name of the body part to be touched. This can add an interesting dimension to the game and give the teacher a greater degree of flexibility in evaluating the performance of the children as far as body-awareness is concerned.

The above games are among the almost unlimited number of those that can be used for purposes of developing body-awareness in children. The teacher can use these as a basis and devise various versions of each of them. In addition, the creative person can invent many of his or her own games using the above games as a guide. It is also recommended that children be encouraged to think up games on their own after playing some of the games that have been recommended here.

Rhythmic Activities

Looby Loo

Verse

1. Here we dance Looby Loo, here we dance Looby Light,
2. Here we dance Looby Loo, all on a Saturday night.
3. I put my right hand in, I take my right hand out,
4. I give my right hand a shake, shake, shake, and turn myself about.

(turn around in place)

I put my left hand in, etc.

I put my right foot in, etc.

I put my left foot in, etc.

Action: The children form a single circle with hands joined. On lines 1 and 2 of the verse the children walk three steps into the circle and three steps back, and repeat. As the rest of the lines are sung, the children do the actions indicated by the words. For example, with "I put my right hand in," they lean forward, extend the right hand and point it toward the center of the circle. At the end of each verse the children repeat the first verse again, taking three steps in and three steps out. The procedure can be continued with other parts of the body as desired, ending with "I put my whole self in," and so on. (Take a short jump in.)

Comment: In a discussion before participation in this activity the teacher can be sure the children are aware of the body part and when to activate it. In addition, the activity can serve well as an evaluative device for the teacher to see how well the children are aware of the various body parts.

Did You Ever See a Lassie?

Verse

1. Did you ever see a lassie, a lassie, a lassie?
2. Did you ever see a lassie go this way and that?
3. Go this way and that way, go this way and that way.
4. Did you ever see a lassie go this way and that?

Action: The children form a circle and one child is chosen to be the leader and stands in the center. On Line 3 of the verse the leader goes through some sort of motion and the children in the circle follow. This continues with different children going to the center of the circle. When a boy is the leader, "laddie" is substituted for "lassie."

Comment: When the teacher evaluates this activity with the children after the participation phase of the lesson, questions for discussion could be the names of the parts of the body that "went this way and that way."

Diddle Diddle Dumpling

Verse
1. Diddle Diddle Dumpling, my son John,
2. Went to bed with one shoe on.
3. Yes, one shoe off, and one shoe on,
4. Diddle Diddle Dumpling, my son John.

Action: The children can be in any formation. On the first line they can either clap hands, knees, or thighs, or any other body part. On the second line they can pretend to sleep with motions such as placing their heads on their hands. On the third line they hop on one foot to indicate they have a shoe off. On the fourth line they repeat the action of the first line.

Comment: In a discussion prior to playing the game, the teacher and the children can determine which body part is to be clapped, and on which foot the shoe will be. During the game, the teacher can determine easily which children are having difficulty following the instructions.

Big Bee

Verse
1. Up on toes, back on heels.
2. Hands on head, see how it feels.
3. Bend at the waist, touch your knees.

4. Skip around if you please.
5. Keep on skipping around the ring.
6. Look out for the Big Bee sting.

Action: All the children except the one who is *Big Bee* form a circle. Big Bee stands inside the circle and close to the children in the circle. The children execute the action indicated in the verse as they sing or chant it. On line 4 they skip around the circle clockwise. Big Bee walks around in the circle counterclockwise. At the end of the last word of the verse all of the children in the circle stoop down. Big Bee tries to tag (sting) one of the children before that child has assumed the stooping position. A new Big Bee is selected and the activity continues.

Comment: After explaining and discussing the actions that the children are to execute, the extent to which they are able to identify the various body parts concerned can be observed. In evaluating the activity with the children the teacher can ask where a child was *stung*, "On the arm?" "On the leg?" etc.

Clap and Tap

As mentioned previously, some of the activities are presented in story form which have been developed for the purpose of using physical education experiences to improve upon listening and reading. *Clap and Tap* is such an activity.[6]

> *Clap and Tap*
> I clap with my hands.
> Clap, clap, clap.
> I tap with my foot.
> Tap, tap, tap.
> I point my toe.
> And around I go.
> Clap, clap, clap.
> Tap, tap, tap.

Comment: The teacher can read the story to the children, then during participation he can see how well they follow the body

---

[6]James H. Humphrey, *Learning to Listen and Read Through Movement* (Deal, New Jersey, Kimbo Educational, 1974): p. 69.

movement directions. The teacher and children can make up their own tune for accompaniment. If the teacher wants to extend the story to the reading task he can give a printed copy to each child. Or, this procedure can be used originally, depending upon the ability of the children. The reading level of this selection is 1.4, which means fourth month of first grade.

Creative Rhythms

It should be recalled that in the preceding chapter creative rhythms were highly recommended on the basis that when a child is able to use his body freely there is a strong likelihood that there will be increased body-awareness. The following is an example of this in story form.[7]

> *The Growing Flowers*
> Flowers grow.
> First they are seeds.
> Be a seed.
> Grow like a flower.
> Grow and grow.
> Keep growing.
> Grow tall.
> Now you are a flower.

Comment: The teacher can carefully observe the movements of the children with reference to the body parts used in the growing flowers. "Did we use our arms? Our legs?" and so on. A drum or suitable recording can be used as accompaniment.

Self-testing Activities

One of the main values in the use of self-testing activities in compensatory physical education is that most of them are individual in nature. Thus, the teacher can have children practice alone those activities which will help eliminate their identified perceptual-motor deficiencies.

---

[7]James H. Humphrey, *Learning to Listen and Read Through Movement*, p. 67.

Axial Movements

Axial movements, or nonlocomotor movements, refer to bending and stretching and twisting and turning and the like. These kinds of movements are ordinarily performed with a part of the body remaining as a fixed base to the surface area. However, they can be done with parts of the body or the whole body in gross movement. For example, twisting can be combined with a locomotor movement to avoid being hit in a game such as dodge ball.

Comment: The teacher might have the children dispersed around the activity area and call out questions that require the use and identification of a body part using axial movement. For example, "Where can we bend?" (wrist, elbow, knee, waist) Bending can be performed at one of these segments and the child can identify the place as he does it. This approach can be expanded in many ways, and the teacher is limited only by his or her imagination and ingenuity.

Measuring Worm

The child extends his body along the floor in a straight line face down. His weight is supported by his hands and toes. With arms and legs extended he takes very short steps until his feet reach his hands. He then moves ahead on his hands with very short "steps" until his body is extended again. He continues to do this for a specified distance.

Comment: It should be brought to the attention of the child how he is using his hands and feet to move along like a measuring worm. In discussing this activity with children, the uses of the body parts, hands, arms, feet and legs are discussed. During the activity the teacher can see how each child reacts to directions. Sometimes children confuse hands and arms and feet and legs.

Spanker

The child lies on his back and raises his body by pushing up with his feet and hands. He walks along in this position on hands and feet. He raises first one hand and then the other as he taps (spanks) himself.

Comment: The hands and feet are identified in terms of their coordinated use. As the child becomes more proficient in the activity the teacher can give instructions to *spank* the body in different places, such as thigh, head, etc.

Squat Thrust

From a standing position the child assumes a squatting stance, placing his hands on the surface area to the outside of his legs with the palms flat and the fingers forward. This is count number 1. Switching the weight to the hands and arms, then the child extends his legs sharply to the rear until his body is straight. The weight of the body is now on the hands and the balls of the feet. This is count number 2. On count number 3 the child returns to the squatting position, and on count number 4 the child returns to the erect standing position.

Comment: The child is able to see the function of certain body parts as the weight is shifted. After directions are given for the performance of the activity the teacher can notice how well they are followed with reference to the correct position of the body parts concerned.

Turk Stand

The Turk Stand may be presented in story form as follows:[8]

The Little King
In a far away land across the sea lives a Little King.
This Little King stands straight and tall.
He folds his arms in front of him.
He crosses one foot in front of the other.
He sits down slowly.
Now the Little King wants to get up.
He keeps his arms the same way.
He keeps his feet the same way.
He rises in this way.
Now he stands straight again.

---

[8]James H. Humphrey, *Learning to Listen and Read Through Movement*, p. 59.

Comment: The teacher can observe how well the children execute the movement after listening to the story, and thus use it as a diagnostic technique.

Giraffe Walk

This activity can be presented in story form as follows:[9]

George Giraffe
There is a tall animal in a far away land.
He has a long neck.
His name is George Giraffe.
You could look like him if you did this.
Place your arms high over your head.
Put your hands together.
Point them to the front.
This will be his neck and head.
Now walk like George Giraffe.
This is how.
Stand on your toes.
Walk with your legs straight.

Comment: The teacher might use something like the following simulated teaching-learning situation with the children after the story has been read and a child has tried the activity.

TEACHER: Wasn't that interesting how Johnny showed us how George Giraffe looked ? (Children respond.) What do you think George Giraffe looked like [from what Johnny did?] (Children respond.) What did Johnny do to look tall like George Giraffe? What did Johnny do to have a long neck like George Giraffe? (Children.) Can someone else make a long neck? (Children demonstrate.) Oh, you are *all* very good at making long necks. Particularly Jimmy. How did Johnny walk to be like George Giraffe? Can someone show us? (Children demonstrate.) What do you have to do to walk like George Giraffe? (Children respond.) Is it easy to pretend to be like George Giraffe? Let's try it and find out

---

[9]James H. Humphrey, *Learning to Listen and Read Through Movement*, p. 48.

(All children demonstrate.) That was very good. You all looked like giraffes. I saw Fred moving his thumbs so it looked like George Giraffe had ears. Let's all try that. (Children demonstrate.)

As in the case of any of the physical education content stories, the teacher can use this one for purposes of reading as well as listening, depending upon the ability level of the children.

Chapter 5

LATERALITY AND DIRECTIONALITY

IT was indicated in Chapter 3 that laterality and directionality are inherent aspects of body-concept. Thus, progress towards greater differentiation within the body-concept and function begins with the learned ability to discriminate between the left and right sides of the body.[1] It has been suggested that the bilaterally symmetrical placement of the limbs, the sense receptors, and the nerve pathways play a significant part in this process.[2] As the child develops a preference for handedness or footedness, it becomes easier for him to distinguish between the two sides of his body. As laterality develops the child begins to apply his learned concepts of *right* and *left* in the location of near objects.[3] The progression here is not automatic, since the learning of *directionality* is preceded by the complex process of learning to integrate the visual information of external objects with the established kinesthetic awareness on which the child has built his concept of *laterality*.[4] Thus, development of laterality precedes development of directionality since the child learns to translate the right-left discrimination within himself into right-left discrimination among objects outside himself.[5]

Laterality can be described as an internal realization that the body has spatially oriented parts such as a right and left side, a front and back, which must be coordinated. *Directionality* is an external referent by which the child learns to use the horizontal and vertical coordinates in the environment for relating himself

---

[1]P. R. Morris and H. T. A. Whiting, *Motor Impairment and Compensatory Education* (Philadelphia, Lea & Febiger, 1971): p. 224.

[2]Newell C. Kephart, *The Slow Learner in the Classroom* (Columbus, Ohio, Charles E. Merrill, 1960).

[3]P. R. Morris and H. T. A. Whiting, *Motor Impairment and Compensatory Education* (Philadelphia, Lea & Febiger, 1971): p. 224.

[4]Newell C. Kephart, *The Slow Learner in the Classroom*, (Columbus, Ohio, Charles E. Merrill, 1960).

[5]Newell C. Kephart, *The Slow Learner in the Classroom*, (Columbus, Ohio, Charles E. Merrill, 1960).

to other objects in space.[6] Or, stated in another way, directionality in space is the ability to project outside of the body the laterality which the child has developed within himself.

Evidence to support the value of the use of training for laterality and directionality is somewhat scarce; however, a couple of examples of such research is reported here. In one such study Lipton[7] investigated perceptual-motor development and reading readiness using 90 first grade children equated on the variables of age, height, and weight. Two groups designated as experimental and control were exposed to two programs, one of which emphasized directionality for a 12-week period. The control group participated in the conventional physical education program, while the other group participated in an experimental physical education program. Significant improvements were reported favoring the experimental group. It was concluded that the experimental physical education program emphasizing directionality is more effective than a conventional program in developing perceptual-motor skills and reading readiness in first grade children.

In another study conducted by August,[8] a physical education program emphasized development of laterality and directionality. The 120 kindergarten subjects in the study were divided randomly into two groups of 60 each. I. Q. range for the groups was 90-130. Using a battery of skill tests and academic readiness tests, the investigator sought to determine the effect of 36 lessons on perceptual-motor development as compared with an equal number of conventional physical education lessons. Although both groups made significant gains in perceptual-motor development, neither was better than the other. This could be interpreted to mean that since the group in conventional physical education did as well there was no need for the structured perceptual-motor experiences.

[6]Mary W. Moffitt, "Play as a Medium for Learning," *Journal of Health, Physical Education and Recreation,* June 1972.

[7]E. D. Lipton, "A Perceptual-Motor Development Program's Effect on Visual Perception and Reading Readiness of First Grade Children," *Research Quarterly,* October 1968.

[8]I. August, "A Study of the Effect of a Physical Education Program on Reading Readiness, Visual Perception and Perceptual-Motor Development in Kindergarten Children," Doctoral Dissertation, New York University, New York, N. Y., 1969.

DETERMINING PROBLEMS OF LATERALITY
AND DIRECTIONALITY

Since laterality and directionality are inherent aspects of body-concept, some of the methods for detecting deficiencies in body-awareness mentioned in the previous chapter also apply here. In addition, it may be noted that the child is inclined to use just the dominant side of his body. Also confusion may result if the child is given directions for body movements which call for a specific direction in which he is to move.

In activities that require a child to run to a given point, such as a base, he may tend to veer away from it. Or, he may not perceive the position of other children in a game and, as a consequence, may run into them frequently. These are factors that teachers can observe in children in their natural play environment, or in their movements about the classroom.

Some teachers have indicated that they have had success with a specific test of laterality.[9] This test is given on a four-inch wide walking board which is two feet in length. The child tries to walk forward, backward and sideways, right to left and left to right, while attempting to maintain his balance. It is suggested that a child with a laterality problem will experience difficulty moving one of the ways sideward, ordinarily from left to right.

ACTIVITIES INVOLVING LATERALITY
AND DIRECTIONALITY

Generally speaking, a relatively large number of physical education activities involve some aspect of lateralness, while a more moderate number are concerned with directionality. Some physical education activities involve *unilateral* movements; those performed with one side or part of the body. Many physical education activities provide for *bilateral* movement. This means that both sides or segments of the body are in action simultaneously in the same manner. *Cross-lateral* movement is involved

---

[9]Eugene Roach and Newell C. Kephart, *The Purdue Perceptual-Motor Survey* (Columbus, Ohio, Charles E. Merrill, 1966).

when segments of the body are used simultaneously but in a different manner. Many activities are concerned with changing direction which is likely to involve directionality. The physical education activities that follow have been selected because they contain certain inherent experiences in laterality and/or directionality. Also, in some of the activities, these inherent experiences are more pronounced and receive more emphasis than might be the case with certain other activities.

Game Activities

Zigzag Run

The group is divided into teams. The teams form rows behind a starting line. Four ten pins, or other objects, are placed in a line four feet apart in front of each team. On a signal, the first child on each team runs to the right of the first pin and to the left of the second pin, and so on, in a zigzag fashion, going around the last pin. He returns to place in the same manner. The second child proceeds as the first child. If a child knocks down a pin, he must set it up before he continues. The team finishing first wins.

Comment: This activity gives children practice in changing direction as they run around the objects. The teacher can observe closely to notice the children who are having difficulty performing the task.

Circle Run

In this game the players form a circle and stand about six feet apart. All face counterclockwise. On a signal all start to run, keeping the general outline of the circle. As they run, each player tries to pass the runner in front of him on the outside. A player passing another tags the one passed and the one passed is out of the race. The last person left in the circle wins. On a designated signal from the teacher the circle turns around and runs in a clockwise direction. This may occur at the discretion of the teacher. (As a general policy children should not be eliminated from an activity. However, this is a strenuous, rapid-moving activity and a player is soon back in the game because of the short playing time.)

Comment: Signals the teacher can use for changing directions are *forward* and *backward* or *front* and *back*. The teacher can observe those children who react slowly to the directions and how quickly they make the change after they do react. This is a good activity for helping children identify the words that mean a change in direction from front to back.

Corn Race

This is a modern version of a game that goes back into the history of our country. In early times while adults were husking corn the children played games with the ears of corn. The group is divided into a number of rows. In front of each row a circle about three feet in diameter is drawn on the playing surface to represent a corn basket. Straight ahead beyond each of the corn baskets, four smaller circles are drawn about ten feet apart. In each of the four small circles is placed an object representing an ear of corn. These objects may be blocks, beanbags or the like. At a signal, the first person in each row runs to the small circles in front of, and in line with, his row, picks up the corn one ear at a time, and puts all the ears into the corn basket. The second person takes the ears from the corn basket and replaces them in the small circles. The third person picks them up and puts them in the basket, and the game proceeds until all members have run and returned to their places.

Comment: This activity provides an opportunity to move forward and backward and to place objects in the process. The teacher should take note of those children who may be confused about their particular task. Assistance can be given those children who need it, either by the teacher or by other children.

Go and Stop

The children stand in dispersed fashion around the activity

area with one person designated as the leader. The leader points in a given direction and says "Hop that way." Or the leader may say, "Skip to the wall." When the leader calls out, "Stop!" all of the children must stoop down. The idea is not to be the last one down. The last person down has a point scored against him and the game continues for a specified period of time.

Comment: In the early stages of this game it might be a good idea for the teacher to be the leader so he can control the various calls. The teacher can observe those children who are able to go immediately in the direction the leader specifies. The teacher should be on the alert to watch for those children who look at another child before making a movement. This can suggest that these children are having difficulty in following the directions.

Ostrich Tag

The children are dispersed around the activity area. One child selected to be *It* attempts to tag one of the children who may protect himself from being tagged by standing in ostrich fashion. That is, he may stand on one foot with his hands behind his back to emulate an ostrich. The other leg is swung back and forth to help maintain balance. If *It* tags a child before he is in this position or after he has moved, that child becomes *It*.

Comment: Before the game starts the teacher can indicate to the children on which foot they are to stand. The teacher can then take note if they are standing on the designated foot. The teacher might also take note of those children who are having difficulty in maintaining balance when standing on one foot.

Changing Seats

Enough chairs for all the children in the group are placed side by side in about four or five rows. The children sit alert, ready to move either way. The teacher calls, "Change right!" and each child moves into a seat on his right. When the teacher calls, "Change left!" each child moves left. The child at the end of the row who does not have a seat to move to must run to the other end of his row to sit in the vacant seat there.

Comment: The teacher can bring excitement to the game by the quickness of commands or unexpectedness by calling the same direction several times in succession. After each signal the first row of children who all find seats may score a point for that row. This is a good activity to help the children learn the distinction between left and right, and to listen to the terms that designate the direction. The teacher should observe those children who move in the wrong direction on signal. Special attention should be given by the teacher when the same signal is called several times in succession. By this careful observation, it can be determined whether or not certain children actually know the directions or are guessing which signal the teacher will give.

Over and Under Relay

The children form several rows, an equal number in each. The first child in each row is given a ball or other object that can be passed to the children behind. At a signal the first child hands the object over his head to the second child; the second child passes it back between his legs to the third child; the third child passes it back over his head, etc. When the last child receives the object, he runs to the head of his row and the same procedure is followed. This procedure continues until the first child returns to the head of his row. The row first completing the circuit wins the game.

Comment: This activity gives the children an opportunity to pass an object in a backward direction while at the same time changing the direction. The teacher can have the children call out "over" or "under" as the case may be so that they can become familiar with the meaning. The terminology can be changed to *up* and *down* if the teacher so desires.

Change Circle Relay

The group is arranged in rows. Three circles are drawn on the surface area a given distance in front of each row. In the circle to the left of each row three objects are placed. These objects can be ten pins or anything that can be made to stand upright. The first child runs to the circle and moves the objects to the next circle; the second child moves them to the last circle, and then each succeeding child repeats this process. That is, the objects are moved from the first circle to the second circle to the third circle, and then back to the first circle. All of the objects must remain standing. If one falls, the last child to touch it must return and set it up. The activity is complete when all players on a team have had an opportunity to change the objects from one circle to another.

Comment: The number of objects can be varied and the activity can be started with just one object. This activity gives the children an opportunity to execute change in direction by placing objects in specified places. If the teacher desires, the circles can be labeled with *left, center*, and *right*.

Dodge Ball

There are many types of Dodge Ball and the three examples that are given here are presented in sequential order. That is, they progress from a simple to complex form of activity. The games presented here are *Roll Dodge, Circle Dodge*, and *Chain Dodge*, all of which are played in circle formation.

Since there are many ways of organizing dodge ball games, a comment about organization seems appropriate at this point. The kind of organization I personally prefer involves dividing the large group into about four smaller groups. Each small group becomes the *dodgers* for a specified period of time while the other three groups are the *throwers*. Each succeeding small group takes its place as dodgers. Each time a person in the group is hit with the ball, it counts a point against his group, and the group with the lowest score, after all four groups have been dodgers, is the winner. This form of organization prevents any child from being eliminated after he has been hit.

The game of Roll Dodge has a circle of throwers with a group of dodgers in the circle. Emphasis is placed *only* on dodging. The throwers *roll* the ball back and forth across the surface area as rapidly as they can while the dodgers try to dodge the ball.

In Circle Dodge the organization is the same as for Roll Dodge, except that the emphasis is placed on both dodging and attempting to strike a dodger. The ball is thrown rather than rolled, and the children can use either an underarm or sidearm throwing pattern.

In Chain Dodge the dodgers make a *chain* by forming a row. Each player gets a firm hold around the waist of the player in front of him. The only person eligible to be hit in the chain is the person at the end of the chain. Any type of throwing pattern can be used. The throwers must move the ball rapidly to each other in various parts of the circle in order to make a hit, and the chain must move in such a way as to protect the child on the end of the chain. If the last person is hit, the game stops temporarily while he goes to the front of the chain, with the previous next-to-last player becoming the player on the end of the chain. The same scoring method prevails.

Comment: Dodge ball, and its variations, provide excellent opportunities for the child to change directions and to try to make a judgment on a change of direction from which an object (ball) is approaching. Also, the throwers must make judgments of direction as they attempt to hit a moving target (dodger). The teacher should be alert to observe those children who have difficulty with any of the tasks required in dodge-ball type games.

Streets and Alleys

This game is depicted in a simulated teaching-learning situation. In this illustration the teacher is integrating the game with pedestrian safety in social studies as well as utilizing its inherent aspects of laterality and directionality.

The class forms into four columns. The columns stand far enough apart so that the children can join hands with the members of the column next to them. The spaces between the columns are the streets. The teacher or a child acting as the leader stands in front of the group. One child is selected to be the chaser and another child is selected to be *It*. They stand near the leader at the start of the game. At a signal from the leader the chaser runs after *It*, who may run up and down the streets (spaces or aisles between the columns). The leader calls "Streets," and the members of the columns take the hands of the members in the columns next to them. Should the leader call out, "Alleys" the columns turn to the right and take the hands of the persons behind. The chaser and *It* run up and down the streets and alleys as the leader calls the changes. If the chaser tags *It*, a new chaser and *It* are selected and the game continues. The success of the game is dependent upon the leader calling "Streets" or "Alleys" at the proper time.

TEACHER: Boys and girls, we have been reading about Sally and Ann and how they looked up and down Pleasant Street for the boys who hid their dolls. Do you remember anything else they did?

PUPIL: They also looked up and down Pleasant Street on their way to Mrs. Hill's store.

TEACHER: Yes. We have also been discussing how we should look up and down all streets before crossing them. We decided that this is a very good rule to follow. Now, today we are going to play a game called Streets and Alleys. When you change positions in this game you may think of it as being like a stop light, and you must be careful to go with the light. (*Teacher continues.*) I will give the directions the first time and later someone else may give them. We will need a chaser and an *It* and about four rows of players. The rows of players will stand facing the leader. The rows should stand far enough apart so they can take the hands of the people beside them with their arms outstretched. The rows must also leave enough space in back of them so they will be able to turn and take the hands in the same manner. When the leader calls, "Streets," the rows of players take hands facing the leader. The leader calls, "Go" to the chaser, who tries to catch *It*. The chaser and *It* run up and down the streets. When the leader calls, "Alleys" the rows of players turn to their right and take the hands of the players who were behind them. The chaser and *It* have to change and run up and down between the alleys. When *It* is caught, the chaser may become *It* or other players may be chosen. The game may be played until time is called or until everyone has had a turn.

(*On the basis of this explanation, the teacher has the children organize the game. They do so with further teacher guidance and then participate in it for a time. The teacher then evaluates it with them.*)

TEACHER: You seemed to enjoy playing the game, but are there some things you think we might do to improve it?

PUPIL: All rows need to turn at the same time.

PUPIL: Your arms get too tired when you hold them up so long.

TEACHER: What could we do about that?

PUPIL: We could just hold our arms up when "Streets" or "Alleys" is called, and when we turn.

TEACHER: That seems like a good idea. I noticed that your arms began to sag.

PUPIL: I went too fast and couldn't slow down and bumped into people when they made an alley out of the street.

TEACHER: Yes, I noticed that, Fred. Remember we said at the beginning that you should think of the change as a stop light and be sure to go with the light. What should we do about that?

PUPIL: Well, for one thing we might slow down when we thought the leader was going to call out "Streets" or "Alleys."

TEACHER: Yes. Why?

PUPIL: Well, it's like racing to try to cross the street when the light is green and you don't know how long it has been green.

TEACHER: You mean you should make sure the light is not going to turn red before you get across.

PUPIL: Yes. It's like when my father drives his car. He says he does not speed up when he comes to a green light because it might change to red. When you are crossing the street, you might be in the middle and the light would turn red.

TEACHER: You have given some good ideas. I hope that you will think of these things when you cross Vine Street across from our school when you go home for lunch at noon. We may try this game another time, and I would like to have you think of ways we could improve it to make it a better game.

Weathervane

This activity is also depicted in a simulated teaching-learning situation to show how a teacher might conduct a lesson in directional orientation in a higher order than just left and right. This activity is integrated with science under the general topical area of *The Universe*.

TEACHER: We are going to learn a new game today. I think it will help you to understand better the picture on page 163 in *Find New Neighbors Reader*. Remember, the story was "He Who Thinks Well and Runs Quickly." Does anyone remember what the picture shows?

PUPIL: They were herding buffaloes.

TEACHER: Yes, the picture shows the buffaloes being herded from east to west. I wonder how the Indians knew which was east and which was west?

PUPIL: I know. They could tell by the sun.

TEACHER: Yes, they could tell by the sun. It rises in the east and sets in the west. Could any of you tell which direction was north if you knew where east or west was?

PUPIL: I think the directions always go around the same way.

TEACHER: Very good, Elsie. Then it would look something like this (*The teacher writes north, east, south, and west on the board.*)

TEACHER: Can you tell us on which side of our building the sun rises?

PUPIL: On this side.

TEACHER: How did you know that, Fred?

PUPIL: Because the sun shines in the room in the morning.

TEACHER: Good. That would mean our room is on what side of the building?

PUPIL: I guess the east side.

TEACHER: Yes, and why?

PUPIL: You said the sun rises in the East.

TEACHER: Now I wonder if anyone can tell us which direction is north?

PUPIL: That way.

TEACHER: Fine. Now, Clinton, since you were able to tell us how we could find our directions, will you go to the table at the north end of the room and get the four cards I have put there? You and Charles may place the cards on the walls in the proper directions.

(*While the cards are being placed, the following discussion takes place.*)

TEACHER: Many people need to know directions. Can you

think of anyone we have been studying lately who need to know directions even more than we would?
PUPIL: Pilots.
TEACHER: That's right, Danny. Anyone else?
PUPIL: Navigators on boats and automobile drivers.
TEACHER: Yes, indeed they do. Now, our cards are up. Let's check to see if they are right. Charles and Clinton have placed them correctly. Now all stand. I will be the weatherman for awhile and you will be the weathervanes.
PUPIL: What is a weathervane?
TEACHER: Jean was absent yesterday. Can anyone tell her?
PUPIL: It is something that you see on a building and it turns with the wind and shows the direction of the wind.
TEACHER: Now we are going to see how well you know your directions. When I say, "South," you quickly make a turn like this to the south. Now, for practice, let's try some more directions. Does everyone understand? We will work in teams. Each row is a team. If you jump the wrong way, you will know it because most of you will probably jump in the right direction. The last one in each row can count how many hands are up and each one will be a point against your team.

(*The game proceeds for a short time and the teacher asks how it might be played differently.*)

TEACHER: What is another way that we could play this game?
PUPIL: Instead of jumping we could take steps in the direction.
TEACHER: Shall we try that?

(*The game is played in this manner for a short time.*)

TEACHER: Are there any other ways we could play this game?
PUPIL: We could make a relay out of it like when we had classroom relays during our last physical education period.
TEACHER: Do you have a suggestion as to how we might do this, Don?
PUPIL: You could draw a square in front of each row and write the directions at the sides of each square. We could run up and put a piece of chalk in the place the way the directions go.

(*The relay is organized with the help of the teacher. At the end of the period the teacher evaluates with the class.*)

TEACHER: What were some of the things we learned by playing this game?
PUPIL: You can tell the east and west by the sun.
PUPIL: The sun rises in the east.
PUPIL: It sets in the west.
TEACHER: Yes, and we also found that north, east, south and west follow in clockwise rotation. What is opposite north?
PUPIL: South.
TEACHER: And what is opposite west?
PUPIL: East.
TEACHER: Do you understand the picture in your reader better?
PUPIL: Yes. I'll look for the sun in pictures now.
TEACHER: How does the sun help pilots and boat navigators?
PUPIL: They can tell directions from it.
PUPIL: I know another way we could play, by using northeast and southeast.
TEACHER: That sounds like a good idea, Ronald. Suppose you and some of the other boys show us another way to play, using more directions. Maybe we can try it next time.

Rhythmic Activities

Hickory Dickory Dock

Verse
1. Hickory Dickory Dock.
2. The mouse ran up the clock.
3. The clock struck one!
4. Watch the mouse run!
5. Hickory Dickory Dock.

Action: The children form a double circle with partners facing. On line 1 the hands are in front of the body to form pendulums and the arms are swung left and right. On line 2 partners change places with six short running steps. On line 3 they clap hands over head. On line 4 they go back to their original place with six short running steps. On line 5 they swing the arms as in line 1.

Comment: The teacher should observe the smoothness of the

arm movements as the children swing the arms, and whether or not the children are following the directions. After line 2 the positions of the children should be noted to make sure that they have made the correct movement. Certain words, such as *up*, can be emphasized as directional terms.

London Bridge

Verse
1. London Bridge is falling down, falling down, falling down.
2. London Bridge is falling down, my fair lady.

Action: Two children stand facing each other, hands clasped and arms extended overhead to form an arch or bridge. The other players form a line holding hands. These players walk under the bridge. On the words, "my fair lady," the two who have formed the bridge (bridge tenders) let their arms drop, catching the child who happens to be passing under at the time. The bridge tenders then ask him to choose something that each of the tenders represent, such as gold or silver. The player caught stands behind the bridge tender who represents gold or silver as the case may be. The activity proceeds until all have been caught and the side with the most players wins. There should not be too many children in the line in order to avoid a long wait for the children caught.

Comment: This activity gives two children (bridge tenders) an opportunity to focus on the child (object) when they drop their arms to catch the child passing under at the time. The word *down* in the verse can be emphasized. When the teacher evaluates the activity with the children the directions used can be brought out.

How Do'Ye Do, My Partner

Verse
1. How do'ye do, my partner.
2. How are you today?
3. Shall we dance in a circle?
4. I will show you the way.
5. Tra la la la la la, etc. (chorus)

Action: The following actions are performed with the singing accompaniment. A double circle is formed, girls on the outside and boys on the inside. Partners face each other and bow. Partners join inside hands and skip counterclockwise around the circle during the chorus. On the last two measures of the chorus the boys move ahead one person and continue to dance with a new partner.

Comment: Each child gets an opportunity to skip with a partner in a given direction. The teacher should observe closely for those boys who do not move forward to the new partner at the proper time. They must coordinate the timing of the verse with the appropriate time to move ahead one person.

A-Hunting We Will Go

Verse
1. Oh! a-hunting we will go,
2. A-hunting we will go.
3. We'll find a fox and put him in a box,
4. But then we'll let him go.

Action: Either four or six children stand in two lines, partners facing each other. The two partners nearest the front of the room should be designated as the head couple. The head couple join hands and slide four steps down away from the front of the room between the two lines while singing the first line of the verse. The other children clap and sing the accompaniment. On line 2 the head couple slides four steps back to their original position. The head couple then drops hands and the head girl skips around to the right and to the end of her line. The head boy does the same thing to his left. This is done while singing lines 3 and 4. They both meet at the other end of the line. The new head couple follows this procedure and then all succeeding couples become head couples until everyone has had an opportunity to be the head couple. After each couple has had an opportunity to be the head couple, the children all join hands and circle clockwise while singing the entire verse.

Comment: The children who clap and sing the accompaniment must coordinate their tempo with those who are sliding, and vice versa. The children who slide have an opportunity to change direction in a lateral plane upon an auditory clue. The teacher can be on the alert to notice those children who are following directions correctly.

Children's Polka

In the starting position for this dance the children form a single circle. Partners turn and face each other. They join hands and extend the arms to shoulder height. A number of suitable recordings are available for this dance.

Accompaniment Action

Measures 1-2: Partners take two slides toward the center of the circle, and stamp feet three times in place — right, left, right.

Measures 3-4: Partners take two slides back to original position and stamp feet three times.

Measures 5-8: Repeat the action in Measures 1-4.

Measures 9-10: Clap hands against own thighs, clap own hands, and clap partner's hands three times.

Measures 11-12: Repeat the action in Measures 9-10.

Measure 13: Extend the right foot to the side with the toe down. Hold the right elbow in the left hand and shake the right forefinger at partner three times.

Measure 14: Same as Measure 13 except that the position is reversed with left foot and left hand.

Measures 15-16: Each person turns around with four running steps and then stamps feet three times — right, left, right.

Comment: This dance provides many opportunities for the children to change direction while at the same time performing a coordinated movement with the hands, such as clapping one's hands and one's partner's hands. As the children learn the activity, the teacher can stress the terms *right* and *left* since they are used as directions for sliding. In all structured rhythmic activities such as those preceding, the teacher might take note of those children who are depending upon others for directions. This could indicate that these children are having more pronounced problems of laterality and/or directionality. Thus, structured rhythmic activities can serve as a diagnostic technique.

Rhythmic Activities Devised by the Teacher

Creative teachers can develop their own rhythmic activities and utilize movements that they desire and that are not included in many of the structured activities. In this way the teacher can "tailor-make" a rhythmic activity for a specific purpose. The following original verse which indicates movements to be made is an example.

> Point to the left.
> Now point to the right.
> Now turn around with all your might.
> Take one step forward.
> Now take one step back
> Now everyone be a jumping jack.
> Point your arms out.
> Point your toes in.
> Now give yourself a little spin.
> Now turn your head.
> Now bend your knees.
> Now buzz around like a hive of bees.

Comment: It is an interesting practice to have the children with the guidance of the teacher also create experiences along the above lines. It has been my personal experience that activities of this nature are likely to be of extreme value because they are devised to meet the needs of children in a specific situation.

Self-testing Activities

The description of self-testing activities given in Chapter 3 suggested that these kinds of activities are those which are based upon the child's desire to test his ability in such a way that he attempts to better his performance, and further, that for the most part these activities involve competing against oneself and natural forces. This is a broad description and many kinds of experiences can satisfactorily be classified in this category. The activities involving laterality and directionality that are included here will be drawn from the classifications of locomotor skills, auxiliary skills, ball handling activities, balance beam activities, stunt activities and tumbling activities.

Locomotor Skills

There are five basic types of locomotor movements; walking, running, leaping, jumping and hopping, and three combinations which are galloping, skipping and sliding. The first five of these are performed with an even rhythm and the last three are done with an uneven rhythm.

As a child moves over the surface area, the proficiency of performance of these movements is dependent upon the degree of skill involved in the execution of such movements. Thus, the *locomotor skills* require a certain amount of strength and the development of the important sensorimotor mechanics that are concerned with balance. They also require various degrees of neuromotor coordination for proficient performance.

All of the locomotor skills should be learned by elementary school children regardless of whether or not they have any kind of perceptual-motor deficiency. The reason for this is that these skills comprise the basic requirements for proficiency of performance in the activities contained in a well-balanced physical education program. Teachers should have certain basic knowledge about the locomotor skills so that they will be alert to improve performance in these skills. The following generalized information is intended for this purpose. Special comments will be made about those skills in which laterality and/or directionality are important factors.

WALKING. Walking involves transferring the weight from one foot to the other and is the child's first experience with bipedal locomotion. The walk is started with a push-off backward against the surface area with the ball and toes of the foot. After this initial movement the leg swings forward from the hip, the heel of the other foot is placed down, the outer half of the foot next, and then the next push-off is made with the toes pointing straight ahead.

Comment: Walking is used in such physical education activities as walking to rhythmical accompaniment, combining the walk with other movements in various dance activities, walking about in singing games, and walking around a circle preparatory to the start of a circle game. At one time *marching* was a part of many physical education programs. However, as physical education objectives changed, this activity became practically extinct because it did not appear to meet any of these objectives. While it is not necessarily recommended here that marching be reinstated as a physical education activity, it can nonetheless be of use in certain aspects of the development of laterality and directionality. That is, the children can be afforded the opportunity to change directions at the signal of the teacher as different forms of directions of movement are called.

RUNNING. As in the case of walking, running involves transferring the weight from one foot to the other, but the rate of speed is increased. The ball of the foot touches the surface area first and the toes point straight ahead. The body is momentarily suspended in the air when there is no contact with the surface area. This differs from the walk, in which contact with either foot is maintained with the surface area. In the run there is more flexion at the knee which involves a higher leg lift. There is also a higher arm lift with flexion at the elbow reaching an angle of about ninety degrees. In running there is more of a forward body lean than in walking and in both cases the head points straight ahead. In many instances the child who has not been taught to run correctly will violate certain mechanical principles by having a backward rather than forward lean, by carrying the arms too high, and by turning the head to the side rather than looking straight ahead.

Comment: Running is probably the most used of all the locomotor skills in physical education, particularly as far as most game activities are concerned. In running activities, as in the case of walking, the teacher can have the children respond to directional signals. The child must react quicker because of the speeding up of the movement.

LEAPING. Like walking and running, leaping is performed with an even rhythm, and is like a slow run with one essential difference. That is, push-off is up and then forward, with the feeling of suspension "up and over." The landing should be on the ball of the foot with sufficient flexion at the knee to absorb the shock.

JUMPING. The jump is accomplished by pushing off with both feet and landing on both feet, or pushing off with one foot and landing on both feet. Since absorption of shock is important in the jump, the landing should be with knees flexed and on the balls of the feet.

Comment: Children can compete against their own performance in individual jumping. This can be done with the standing broad jump (taking off and landing on both feet), or the long jump (running to a point and taking off on one foot and landing on both feet). The standing broad jump is an example of a good bilateral movement inasmuch as the arms and legs work together to propel the body forward.

HOPPING. The skill of hopping involves taking off and landing on the same foot. Hopping from a standing position is a more complex aspect of the jump because the body is elevated from the surface area by the action of only one foot. Not only is greater strength needed for the hop, but also a more refined adjustment of balance is required because of the smaller base of support.

Comment: Hopping, as such, is not used frequently as a specific skill in many physical education activities. Exceptions include such dance steps as the schottische, which involves a pattern of *step-step-step-hop-step-hop-step-hop*, or the hopping relay, in which children hop to a point on one foot and return on the other foot. In addition, it should be obvious that such games as hopscotch require skill in the ability to hop.

Even though hopping is not a specific skill used in most physical education activities, one of the more important reasons why children should become proficient in this skill is that it can help them regain balance in any kind of activity when they have temporarily "lost their footing." When this occurs, the child can use the hop to keep his balance and remain in an upright position while getting the temporarily incapacitated foot into action. In preparing for the hop children should be taught to shift the weight to the hopping foot before releasing the other foot from the surface area. This helps to get the weight distribution over the smaller base of support more easily. This is particularly important in mounting the balance beam as we shall see later.

GALLOPING. The skill of galloping is a combination of the basic patterns of walking and leaping, and is performed with an uneven rhythm. It can be explained by pretending that one foot is injured. A step is taken with the lead foot, but the "injured" foot can bear very little weight and is brought up only behind the other one and not beyond it. A transfer of weight is made to the lead foot, and thus a fast limp is really a gallop.

Comment: Galloping is a skill that does not have prevalent use as a specific skill in most physical education activities. An exception is its use as a fundamental rhythm when children become "galloping horses" to appropriate rhythmical accompaniment. One of the most important factors in learning how to gallop is that it helps children to be able to change direction in a forward or backward plane more easily, an important accomplishment as far as directionality is concerned. Backward galloping can be done by starting with the lead foot to the back. If a child is proficient in galloping, it is likely he will be more successful in game activities that require a quick forward and/or backward movement for successful performance in that particular activity.

SLIDING. Sliding is much the same as the gallop, but movement is in a sideward direction. One foot is drawn up to the lead foot; weight is shifted from the lead foot to the drawing foot and back again.

Comment: As in the case with other locomotor skills that are uneven in rhythm, sliding is not used frequently as a specific skill in most physical education activities. The important feature of gaining proficiency in the skill of sliding is that it helps the child to be able to change direction skillfully in a lateral plane. When a child has developed the skill of sliding from side to side he does not have to cross his feet, and thus he can change direction laterally much more rapidly.

SKIPPING. Although skipping requires more coordination than galloping, some children will perform variations of the skip when they are about four years of age. With proper instruction, most children should be able to accomplish this movement by age six. Skipping can be taught from the walk. A strong push-off should be emphasized. The push-off should be such a forceful upward movement that the foot leaves the surface area. In order to maintain balance a hop is taken. The sequence is step, push off, hop. The hop occurs on the same foot that was pushing off, and this is the skip. The two actions cause it to be uneven as to rhythm, with a strong or long action (step) and a short one (hop).

Auxiliary Skills

There are certain skills that are not ordinarily classified as either locomotor or axial. However, they are very important in the successful performance of many physical education activities. These skills are arbitrarily identified here as *auxiliary* skills. Among some of the more important skills are: starting, stopping, dodging, pivoting, falling and landing. Three of these, stopping, dodging, and falling are discussed here. For those children who have perceptual-motor deficiencies, and problems of laterality and directionality in particular, these skills are of singular importance.

STOPPING. The skill of stopping is very important because all locomotor movements culminate with this skill. Numerous game activities require quick stopping for successful performance. Two ways of stopping are the *stride* stop and the *skip* stop. The stride stop involves stopping in running stride. There is flexion at the knees and there is a slight backward lean to maintain balance. This method of stopping can be used when the performer is moving at a slow speed. The skip stop should be used when there is fast movement and the performer needs to come to a quick stop. This is accomplished with a hop on either foot, with the opposite foot making contact with the surface area almost simultaneously.

Comment: The teacher can have the children practice stopping from the locomotor skill of running. This can be done on signal. The teacher can be alert to observe proper stopping form, which calls for judgment of running speed on the part of the child.

DODGING. The auxiliary skill of dodging involves changing body direction while running. The knees are bent and the weight is transferred in the dodging direction. This movement is sometimes referred to as *veering* or *weaving*. After a dodge is made the performer can continue in the different direction with a push-off from the surface area with the foot to which the weight was previously shifted.

Comment: The importance of the auxiliary skill of dodging should be obvious as far as laterality and directionality are concerned. The teacher can have children practice this skill by calling out changes in the direction to dodge, such as left and right.

FALLING. In those activities that require an upright position, emphasis, of course, should be on maintaining this position. Nevertheless, there are occasions when a performer loses balance and falls to the surface area. Whenever possible, a fall should be taken in such a way that injury is least likely to occur. One way to accomplish this is to attempt to *break the fall* with the hands. Relaxation and flexion at the joints that put the performer in a *bunched* postion are helpful in avoiding injury when falling to the surface area.

Comment: It is possible that children with perceptual-motor deficiencies, and laterality and directionality problems in particular, may find it difficult to keep in an upright position. Practice in the correct way to make contact with the surface area when falling can take place in connection with the various rolls in tumbling activities. When done in this manner the child is not aware that he is being taught how to fall, thus making this procedure a positive rather than a negative approach.

Ball Handling Activities

As mentioned in chapter three, ball handling activities can be useful in helping children develop eye-hand coordination, timing and bilaterality. The following list of activities is concerned with all of these factors in some way.

STATIONARY BOUNCE. Using both hands, bounce the ball to the surface area and catch it while standing in place. This can be repeated any number of times.

WALKING BOUNCE. Using both hands, bounce the ball to the surface area and catch it while walking.

PARTNER BOUNCE. Using both hands, bounce the ball to a partner who returns it. The distance between partners can be increased as desired.

BOUNCE AROUND. Children form a circle; using both hands, they bounce the ball around the circle, with each child retrieving it and bouncing it to the next. The circle can be made up of any number of children; however, not more than five are recommended, so that each child will get the greatest number of turns.

STATIONARY TAP. Tap the ball with one hand while standing in place. Either hand can be used depending upon the individual child, and the tapping can be repeated any number of times.

THROW AND CATCH. Throw the ball into the air and catch it. The height of the throw can be increased as desired.

BOUNCE-CLAP-CATCH. Bounce the ball to the surface area and clap the hands before catching it.

Balance Beam Activities

Generally speaking, there are two classifications of balance beams — the *high* balance beam and the *low* balance beam. The high balance beam, although adjustable, is ordinarily placed at a height of four feet from the surface area. The width of the high balance beam is four inches. The high balance beam is considered to be the official beam for higher level gymnastic competition.

The low balance beam is ordinarily six to ten inches above the surface area and the width of the beam is two inches. When a four-inch width is used at this height it is generally referred to as a *walking board.* This greater width is often desirable when young children are beginning to learn balance beam activities. All of our discussions here, and the activities that will follow are concerned only with the low balance beam.

There are two types of balance, that is, *static* balance and *dynamic* balance. Static balance is the retention of balance in a stationary position, and dynamic balance is the ability to maintain a position of balance during body movement. We are predominantly concerned here with dynamic balance.

Two important factors need to be considered as general procedures employed in the teaching of balance beam activities. These are *mounting* and *spotting.* In a very large majority of cases the lack of success in balance beam activities is due to the fact that the child mounts the beam incorrectly. The incorrect, but usual, procedure is that the child stands in front of the beam, instead of standing in the correct mounting position *astride* the beam.

When a child stands in front of the beam he must shift his weight forward rather than sideward, and thus mounts the beam in an "off-balance" position. Standing astride the beam, the child places his foot on the beam and then shifts his weight sideward before releasing the opposite foot from the surface area. With this procedure it is much easier to maintain balance while mounting the beam.

There is a tendency for most teachers to *spot* or assist the child from the side rather than from the front or rear. When the *spotter* walks along at the side of the child and holds his hand, there appears to be a psychological tendency for the child to lean in that direction whether he needs assistance or not. This can cause him to lose his balance. For this reason, if the child needs assistance, it is more helpful to him if the spotter walks behind him with his hands on the child's waist, or in front of him with the spotter holding the child's hands. The same situation holds true if the balance beam is placed close to a wall for the purpose of the child using the wall for support. The psychological tendency seems to prevail and the child tends to lean toward the wall. Moreover, the child can inadvertently push away from the wall, causing the balance beam to slide and exposing the child to injury.

The following low balance beam activities are representative of many possibilities suitable for use with elementary school children. These activities can help the child maintain his relationship to gravity, and at the same time help him to develop space awareness and directionality related movements.

FRONT WALK. Walk forward on the beam using any length of step.

BACK WALK. Walk backward on the beam using any length of step.

FRONT AND BACK WALK. Walk forward to the center of the beam using any length of step; turn and continue, walking backward, using any length of step to the end of the beam.

FORWARD FOOT FRONT WALK. Walk forward on the beam with either foot always in front of the other. The lead foot moves forward and the trailing foot comes up to the lead foot but not beyond it.

BACKWARD FOOT BACK WALK. Walk backward on the beam with

either foot always in the lead.

FRONT WALK RETRIEVE OBJECT. Place an object such as a chalkboard eraser or book in the center of the beam. Walk forward, stoop down, pick up the object and continue walking to the end of the beam before dismounting.

FRONT WALK KNEEL. Walk forward to the center of the beam, kneel down until one knee touches the beam, rise to an upright position and continue walking to the end of the beam.

FRONT WALK OBJECT BALANCE. Place an object on the head. Mount the beam and walk the length of the beam while balancing the object on the head.

BACK WALK OBJECT BALANCE. Place an object on the head. Mount the beam and walk backward the length of the beam while balancing the object on the head.

FRONT WALK RETRIEVE AND BALANCE OBJECT. Place an object in the center of the beam. Walk forward to the center of the beam, stoop down and pick up the object, place it on the head, and continue walking to the end of the beam while balancing the object.

FRONT WALK OVER. Have two children hold a piece of string or rope stretched across the center of the beam at a height of about twelve to fifteen inches. Walk forward on the beam, step over the string and continue walking to the end of the beam.

BACK WALK OVER. The same procedure is used as for the Front Walk Over, except that the child walks backward on the beam.

FRONT WALK UNDER. Have two children hold a piece of string or rope stretched across the center of the beam at a height of about three to four feet. Walk forward on the beam, stoop down and go under the string, and then continue walking to the end of the beam.

BACK WALK UNDER. The same procedure is used as for the Front Walk Under, except that the child walks backward on the beam.

Stunts and Tumbling

Stunts may be described as certain kinds of imitations and the performance of a variety of feats that utilize such abilities as balance, coordination, flexibility, agility, and strength. Tumbling involves various kinds of body rolls and body springs that encourage the development of these same abilities. The following activities are representative of those that can be used for the improvement of laterality and directionality.

CRAB WALK. The child sits on the surface area with his knees bent and his hands on the surface area behind his hips. He raises his hips until his trunk is straight. In this position he walks forward and backward or to the side.

Comment: The number of steps taken may be specified with reference to direction. That is, so many steps forward and so many backward. Also, the teacher can call out the directions for the "crab" to pursue; forward, backward, or sideward left or right.

ROCKING CHAIR: Two children sit facing each other, with feet close to the body. Each sits on the feet of the other. They grasp each other just above the elbows and in this position, rock back and forth.

Comment: The children can call out the words *forward* and *back* as they rock.

UP AND DOWN. Two children stand facing each other holding hands. One child stoops down. When he stands the other stoops down.

Comment: They can go up and down any number of times, each time calling out whether they are up or down.

WICKET WALK. The child walks forward and backward or to the side on all fours. The hands are kept flat on the surface area and the knees are straight. The hands are placed far enough apart in front of the feet so that the knees do not bend.

Comment: Directions for the movements can be given by the teacher or by the other children. When children give the directions they can observe the change in direction of the other children.

LOG ROLL. The child assumes an extended prone position with his stomach facing toward the mat. The extended body position along the vertical axis is accomplished by placing the arms over the head along the mat until they are straight. The legs are also extended with the feet together and the toes pointed. The child then uses his head, shoulders, and hips to turn 360 degrees along the mat.

Comment: The child should attempt to roll in a straight line in either direction down the mat. This is a good activity for developing directional movement. The teacher should observe those children who are not rolling in a straight line. This can be improved by keeping the body extended and straight. The child can call out his own movements as he rolls first to one side and then to the other.

FORWARD ROLL. The child assumes a squatting position, his hands placed on the mat, palms flat and fingers forward, a shoulder-width apart. The knees are between the arms, the neck is flexed, and the chin should be close to the chest. The initial movement is given to the body by an extension of the ankle joint so the force is extended at the balls of the feet. This forward motion moves over the arms and hands as the head is lowered and the buttocks raised. The arms are closely bent in order to allow the head to move under the hips without touching the mat. The nape of the neck will come into contact with the mat first, and then the momentum will be transferred to the back, moving, respectively, to the buttocks and the feet. The body should retain the tuck position throughout the activity, and the child should not allow his hands to touch the mat after the original placement at the starting position.

Comment: This is good movement for bilaterality and directionality. If the child continually rolls over his shoulders, have him move his legs to the outside of his elbows, and place the hands a little more than a shoulder-width apart. Instruct children who have difficulty to spread their feet as far apart as possible to perform the roll. Children who need help can be assisted by the teacher lifting them at the nape of the neck and at the shin of the leg.

BACKWARD ROLL. The child assumes the starting position by squatting on the feet, which are approximately a shoulder-width apart. He places his hands, palms up, tightly above his shoulders and keeps his elbows in front of his chest. His thumbs are pointed toward his ears and his fingers pointed backward. If possible, the chin touches the chest. Momentum is created by a loss of the equating balance backward (push with the balls of the feet). The tuck position is maintained as the buttocks, back, hands and feet, respectively, come in contact with the mat. Arms are straightened at the point where the shoulders and hands touch the mat and the buttocks are over the mat. The activity ends with the child on his feet, back in the initial squatting position.

Comment: The child can be assisted by lifting under and grasping each side of his hips. For the child who has difficulty with the activity, have him assume a position on his back and place his hands on the mat as if he were doing the roll. Then have him spread his legs apart and reach over his head with his legs until his toes touch the mat. Next, pick him up under his hips, to give him the "feel" of the activity.

Chapter 6

KINESTHETIC AND
TACTILE PERCEPTION

IN view of the fact that Chapters 6 and 7 deal with
sensory modalities that modify the term *perception,* it seems appropriate to describe briefly the meaning of perception at this
point. The term perception has been described by psychologists
and others in a number of ways; however, these descriptions appear to be more alike than they are different. For example, one
source describes perception as "an individual's awareness of and
reaction to stimuli."[1] A second source refers to it as the "processes
by which the individual maintains contact with his environment."[2] And still another source describes it as the "mental interpretation of the messages received through the senses."[3]

According to Piaget[4] perception is developmental; that is, it
changes with age and experience, and development is continuous
and quantitative. Development of perception occurs in three
major periods: (1) sensorimotor intelligence, which occurs
during the period between birth to about two years, is concerned
with learning to coordinate various perceptions and movements;
(2) the ages from two to about eleven or twelve involve preparation for, and organization of concrete operations, and deals with
the acquisition of language (it is during this period that the child
learns to deal logically with his surroundings); and (3) formal
operations which occur after the age of eleven or twelve, and deal
with the development of abstract and formal systems.

It is suggested that the senses most involved in learning are

---

[1]Robert E. Silverman, *Psychology,* 2nd ed. (New York, Appleton-Century-Crofts, 1974): p.
151.
[2]R. H. Day, *Perception* (Dubuque, Iowa, Wm. C. Brown Company Publishers, 1966): p. 1
[3]Donald C. Cushenbery and Kenneth J. Gilbreath, *Effective Reading Instruction for Slow
Learners* (Springfield, Illinois, Charles C Thomas Publisher, 1972): p. 98.
[4]Jean Piaget, *Les Mecanismes Perdeptifs* (Paris, Presses Universitares de France, 1961).

88

visual perception, *auditory* perception, *tactile* perception, and *kinesthetic* perception.[5] These are the topics for discussion in Chapters 6 and 7.

KINESTHETIC PERCEPTION

As in the case of perception, kinesthesis (or the kinesthetic sense) has been described in various ways by different individuals. However, as in the case of perception, these descriptions appear to be much more alike than different. Some years ago Scott[6] gave a comprehensive definition of kinesthesis as "the sense which enables us to determine the position of the segments of the body, their rate, extent, and direction of movement, the position of the entire body, and the characteristics of total body motion." More recently Silverman[7] has characterized kinesthesis as the "sense that tells the individual where his body is and where and how it moves." In defining kinesthetic perception, Phillips and Summers[8] have called it "the conscious awareness of the individual of the position of the parts of the body during voluntary movement." A later description of kinesthetic perception by Cushenbery and Gilbreath[9] refers to it as the "mental interpretation of the sensation of movement."

In summarizing a number of definitions of the term *kinesthesis*, Oxendine[10] suggests that the following four factors seem to be constant, thus emphasizing the likenesses of the various definitions: (1) position of body segments, (2) precision of movement, (3) balance, and (4) space orientation.

In view of the fact that there may be some confusion with regard to the meaning of the terms *kinesthetic* and *proprioception*, it

[5]Donald C. Cushenbery and Kenneth J. Gilbreath, *Effective Reading Instruction for Slow Learners*, p. 98.
[6]M. Gladys Scott, "Measurement of Kinesthesis," *Research Quarterly*, October 1955.
[7]Robert E. Silverman, *Psychology*, p. 47.
[8]Marjorie Phillips and Dean Summers, "Relation of Kinesthetic Perception to Motor Learning," *Research Quarterly*, December 1954.
[9]Donald C. Cushenbery and Kenneth J. Gilbreath, *Effective Reading Instruction for Slow Learners*, p. 98.
[10]Joseph B. Oxendine, *Psychology of Motor Learning* (New York, Appleton-Century-Crofts, 1968): p. 291.

might be a good idea to comment on it at this point. Singer,[11] a physical educator, maintains that the terms kinesthetic and proprioception generally refer to the *same* sense. He indicates that experimental psychologists usually refer to this sense as *kinesthetic* while physiologists prefer the term *proprioceptive*. This may be a minority point of view with a more prevalent notion being that the kinesthetic receptors are a *subclass* of a larger system of *proprioception*. Armington[12] explains it in the following manner.

> The proprioceptive senses which provide information regarding the orientation and position of the body and its members include two general subclasses, the kinesthetic receptors and the vestibular receptors. The kinesthetic receptors are located in the muscles, tendons and joints where they can provide information about the position and movement of the limbs, head, neck, etc. The vestibular system is closely associated with that of hearing and the ear. Although the receptor mechanisms of the vestibular system are variations of those used for hearing, they provide information regarding the orientation of the body and head, position and balance, and its acceleration through space.

The importance of kinesthetic perception to physical educators should be obvious since all physical education activities involve movement of some sort. Those receptors responsible for informing the body of its conscious change in position as well as the relationship of its parts in space have been demonstrated to be necessary for the smooth movements of skilled act.[13]

TACTILE PERCEPTION

The tactile sense is very closely related to the kinesthetic sense; so much so in fact, that these two senses are oftentimes confused. One of the main reasons for this is that the ability to detect

[11]Robert N. Singer, *Motor Learning and Human Performance* (New York, The Macmillan Company, 1968): p. 73.

[12]John C. Armington, *Physiological Basis of Psychology*, Dubuque, Iowa, Wm. C. Brown Company Publishers, 1966): p. 19-20.

[13]Robert N. Singer, *Motor Learning and Human Performance*, p. 78.

changes in touch (tactile) involves many of the same receptors concerned with informing the body of changes in its position.[14] The essential difference between the tactile sense and the kinesthetic sense may be seen in the definitions of kinesthetic and tactile perception. As stated previously, kinesthetic perception involves the "mental interpretation of the sensation of movement," whereas tactile perception is concerned with the "mental interpretation of what a person experiences through the sense of touch."[15]

The great importance of developing children's tactile perception in physical education is pointed up by Smith[16] in several profound statements. In tracing the development of the tactile sense, she indicates that the end organs of touch in the skin appear to follow the usual cephalocaudal direction of development (from the head to the extremities). The point is made that young children, and those of elementary school age should have numerous opportunities to explore the environment tactilely with all body segments. She further suggests that physical educators might abandon the traditional practice of having the children in sneakers for *all* activity sessions, so that some activities have to be performed barefooted. The reason for this recommendation is that the tactile receptors on the soles of the feet and toes are extremely important for signaling shifts of weight and changes in surface texture. With reference to the latter, it is suggested that activity areas should be surfaced in a variety of ways, allowing for tactile experiences with such surfaces as sand, hard top, natural grass and artificial turf.

In addition to the importance of tactile stimulation as an essential factor for certain movements, another of its dimensions is that concerned with social interaction through tactile *communication*. Thus, the tactile sense not only has physiological and psychological implications, but important sociological implica-

[14]Robert N. Singer, *Motor Learning and Human Performance*, p. 79.
[15]Donald C. Cushenbery and Kenneth J. Gilbreath, *Effective Reading Instruction for Slow Learners*, p. 98.
[16]Hope M. Smith, "Implications for Movement Education Experiences Drawn from Perceptual-Motor Research," *Journal of Health, Physical Education, and Recreation*, April 1970, p. 41.

tions as well. Johnson and Pease[17] call attention to the possibilities of this in the physical education experiences of children. They suggest that better human relations can be obtained through *intrinsic* tactile communication, and cite as examples the utilization of certain physical education activities requiring touch for elementary school children. They would include among such activities dual stunts, dancing and group games. In investigating this phenomenon objectively, Johnson[18] reports that a recent study substantiated the idea that tactile communication in sport provides a basis for the attraction that is necessary for black and white children to form positive relationships. More specifically, her study found that recorded incidents of tactile interaction between black children and white children were equivalent to the recorded incidents of tactile interaction between black children and black children and those between white children and white children.

DETERMINING PROBLEMS OF KINESTHETIC AND TACTILE PERCEPTION

Although there are a number of specific test items that are supposed to measure kinesthesis, the use of such tests may be of questionable value in diagnosing deficiencies in elementary school children. Therefore, the recommendation is that teachers resort to the observation of certain behaviors and mannerisms of children, using some simple diagnostic techniques to determine deficiencies in kinesthetic and tactile sensitivity. The following information is submitted as a generalized guideline to assist the reader in identifying such deficiencies.

Various authorities on the subject suggest that children with kinesthetic and tactile problems possess certain characteristics that may be identifying factors. For example, Frostig[19] has indi-

---

[17]Susan B. Johnson and Dean A. Pease, "Tactile Communication in Sport," *Journal of Health, Physical Education, and Recreation,* February, 1974.
[18]Susan B. Johnson, "The Effects of Tactile Communication in Sport on Changes in Interpersonal Relationships Between Black and White Children, Master's Thesis, Memphis State University, Memphis, Tennessee, 1973.
[19]Marianne Frostig, "Sensory-motor Development," *Special Education,* 57, 2(1968).

cated that "a child who is deficient in kinesthetic and tactile sensitivity will be clumsy and awkward and inefficient in his movements and impaired in getting acquainted with and handling the world of objects." This idea was previously supported by Ayers[20] who suggested that "a child who has difficulty in the use of his hands or his body in attempting to perform unfamiliar motor tasks can benefit from kinesthetic and tactile training."

With reference to the above, the teacher should be on the alert to observe those children who have difficulty with motor coordination; that is, difficulty using the muscles in such a manner that they work together effectively. Such lack of coordination may be seen with children who have difficulty in performing the locomotor skills that involve an uneven rhythm (skipping, galloping and sliding) described in the preceding chapter. Teachers can observe these deficiencies in the natural play activities of children, and the skills themselves can be used as diagnostic techniques in identifying such problems.

Since balance is an important aspect of kinesthesis, simple tests for balance can be administered to determine if there is a lack of proficiency. One such test would be to have the child stand on either foot. Normally, a child should be able to maintain such a position for a period of about ten seconds.

A number of elementary diagnostic techniques for tactile sensitivity can be played in a game type of situation so the child is unaware of being tested. The following list suggests some representative examples, and creative teachers are limited only by their own imagination in expanding the list.

1. Have the child explore the surface and texture of objects in the classroom. Determine if he can differentiate among these objects.
2. Evaluate the child's past experience by having him give the names of two or three hard objects, two or three rough objects, and so on.
3. Some classroom teachers have had successful experience with the *learning box* idea; that is, a listening box for language arts, a math box center and the like. A *touching box*

[20]A. Jean Ayers, "The Development of Perceptual-Motor Abilities: A Theoretical Basis for Treatment of Dysfunction," *American Journal of Occupational Therapy*, XVII, 6.

can be developed with the use of an ordinary shoebox in which are placed different shaped objects and different textured objects. The child reaches into the box without looking, and feels the various objects to see if he can identify them.

ACTIVITIES INVOLVING KINESTHETIC PERCEPTION

Game Activities

Since kinesthetic sensitivity is concerned with the sensation of movement and orientation of the body in space, it is not an easy matter to isolate specific games suited *only* for this purpose. The reason for this, of course, is that practically all games in physical education involve total or near total physical response. That is, active games are concerned with one or more of the locomotor skills as well as many of the auxiliary skills. Therefore, practically all games are of value in the improvement of kinesthetic sensitivity. However, the kinds of games that make the child particularly aware of the movement of certain muscle groups, as well as those where he encounters resistance, are of particular value in helping the child develop a kinesthetic awareness of his body. A couple of games in this classification follow.

Rush and Tug

In this activity there are two groups with each group standing between one of two parallel lines which are about forty feet apart. In the middle of these two parallel lines a rope is laid perpendicular to them. A cloth is tied to the middle of the rope to designate both halves of the rope. On a signal, members of both groups rush to their half of the rope, pick it up and tug toward the group's end line. The group pulling the midpoint of the rope past its own end line in a specified amount of time is the winner. If, at the end of the designated time, the midpoint of the rope has not been pulled beyond either group's line, the group with the midpoint of the rope nearer to its end line is the winner.

Comment: In this game the children experience resistence as they try to pull the opposing group; they also experience the feel of the muscle groups of the arms and legs working together.

Poison

The players form a circle and join hands. A circle is drawn on the activity area inside the circle of players, and about twelve to eighteen inches in front of the feet of the circle of players. With hands joined they pull and tug each other, trying to make one or more persons step into the drawn circle. Anyone who steps into the circle is said to be "poisoned." As soon as a person is poisoned, someone calls out, "Poison!" and the one who is "poisoned" becomes *It* and gives chase to the others. The other players run to various objects of certain material designated as *safety*, such as wood, stone, metal or the like. All of the players tagged are poisoned and become chasers. After those not tagged have reached safety, the leader calls out "Change!" and they must run to another safety point. Those tagged attempt to tag as many others as possible. The game can continue until all but one have been poisoned.

Comment: This activity provides an opportunity for kinesthetic awareness as a child tries to keep from being pulled into the circle. Also surface area resistance may be encountered depending upon the type of surface where the activity takes place.

Rhythmic Activities

As far as kinesthetic sensitivity is concerned, the same situation that applied to game activities could also apply to rhythmic activities. That is, as in the case of game activities, rhythmic activities are concerned with body movement and the position of the body in space. Thus, practically all rhythmic activities would be useful in the improvement of kinesthetic sensitivity. (The reader is referred to the general discussion of the place of rhythmic activities in perceptual-motor development in Chapter 3.) However, and again, as in the case of game activities, there are certain types of rhythmic activities that can make the *child aware of the movements of certain muscle groups.* To this end, I have developed specific rhythmic activities in the form of stories (see Chapter 3) for the purpose of using the physical education experience to improve listening and reading. This procedure has been in favor with language arts specialists for many years as exemplified by the following statement by Beaumont and Franklin:[21] "their kinesthetic sense — the sense of 'feel' they get through their muscles — seems to be highly developed, and it helps some children remember words they would take much longer to learn by looking at or sounding out."

Two of these stories are reproduced here and emphasize the movement of certain muscle groups. The child is alerted to this because the story gives him directions for the movements to be made.

We Dance[22]
We hold hands.
We make a ring.
We swing our arms.
We swing.
We swing.
We take four steps in.
We take four steps out.
We drop our hands.
We turn about.

Around the Ring[23]
Do you know a song about hunting?

---

[21]Florence Beaumont and Adele Franklin, "Who Says Johnny Can't Read?" *Parents Magazine*, June 1955.
[22]James H. Humphrey, *Learning to Listen and Read Through Movement* (Deal, New Jersey, Kimbo Educational, 1974): p. 68.
[23]James H. Humphrey, *Learning to Listen and Read Through Movement*, p. 72.

It is called, "A-Hunting We Will Go."
Here is one way to do it.
Children hold hands in a ring.
Sing these words.
Sing them like you would sing,
   "A-Hunting We Will Go."
Oh! Around the ring we go.
Around the ring we go.
We stop right here.
We clap our hands.
And then sit down just so.

Comment: The teacher can evaluate the experience with the children by questioning them about what they did. Also, the activities can be repeated to see if the children show improvement in understanding the muscle groups involved in the performance of the activities.

Self-testing Activities

Many self-testing activities make the child aware of certain muscle group movements, even resistance. Various tumbling activities previously described involve these kinds of experiences. Also the uneven locomotor skills (skipping, sliding and galloping) are important in the improvement of kinesthetic sensitivity.

Ball handling activities with the use of different sized balls are of value as far as *timing* relates to kinesthetic perception. In addition to those described in Chapter 5, the following are of value.

Bounce-Turn-Catch

Bounce the ball and turn around and catch it before it bounces a second time. At the outset of this activity, it may be a good idea to throw the ball into the air, then turn around to catch it on the bounce. In this variation, the child has more time to turn around before the ball bounces.

Leg-over Bounce

Bounce the ball, swing the leg over it, and catch it. This can be done with either leg, and then the legs can be alternated.

Leg-over Tap

This is the same as the Leg-over Bounce except the child causes the ball to bounce by continuous tapping.

Wall Target Throw

Throw the ball at a wall target, catching it when it returns. The distance can be increased and the size of the target decreased as desired.

As mentioned previously, balance beam activities are an extremely important factor in kinesthesis. Along with those described in the preceding chapter, the following may also be used to advantage in improving kinesthetic sensitivity.

Front Walk Kneel with Leg Extension

Walk forward to the center of the beam, and kneel down until one knee touches the beam. From this position, extend the opposite leg forward until the leg is straight and the heel of the extending leg is touching the beam. Return to the upright position on the beam and continue walking to the end of the beam.

Back Walk Kneel with Leg Extension

The same procedure is used as for the Front Walk Kneel with Leg Extension, except that the child walks backward on the beam.

ACTIVITIES INVOLVING TACTILE PERCEPTION

It was mentioned before that both Frostig and Ayers give strong support to the value of tactile sensitivity training for children who show weakness in this area. With regard to the need for such training, the former suggests that the child needs tactile stimulation through touching and being touched,[24] while the latter also recognizes the vast importance of the major part played by the tactile modality.[25] The physical education activities that follow which involve "touching and being touched," not only apply to tactile stimulation, but also to tactile communication as a means of social interaction, referred to earlier in the chapter.

Game Activities

There are innumerable game activities which provide an opportunity for tactile sensitivity. Some representative examples follow.

Electric Shock

The players form a circle with one player designated as *It* standing inside the circle. *It* attempts to determine where the *electric power* is concentrated. The players in the circle join hands and one player is designated to start the electricity. This player accomplishes this by tightly squeezing the hands of the person on either side of him. As soon as a person's hand is squeezed, he keeps the electricity moving by squeezing the hand of the person next to him. If *It* thinks he knows where the electric power is — that is, whose hand is being squeezed — he calls out that person's name. If *It* has guessed correctly, all of the players in the circle run to a previously designated safety area to avoid being tagged by him. A point is scored against all of those tagged, and the game continues with another player becoming *It*.

Comment: In this situation, the tactile sense becomes a medium of communication as each child's hand is squeezed by another.

---

[24]Marianne Frostig, "Sensory-motor Development," *Special Education* 57, 2 (1968).
[25]A. Jean Ayers, "The Development of Perceptual-Motor Abilities: A Theoretical Basis for Treatment of Dysfunction, *American Journal of Occupational Therapy*, XVII, 6.

Feel and Pass

The children form a circle and face outward with their hands behind them. Articles that have a particular textural characteristic are held by a designated person and passed around the circle from one child to another behind their backs so that they cannot see the articles. One child designated as the last person in the circle receives all of the articles and places them in a container in the order he received them. The children then attempt to describe the articles in the order they received them.

Comment: After the game is played with one circle, there can be several small circles and the articles can be passed to see which circle finishes first. Additional articles can be added as the children gain more proficiency in tactility. The activity can serve as a diagnostic technique since the teacher can note the children who can't identify the articles correctly.

Fish Net

The children are divided into two groups. One group is the net; the other is the fish. At the start, the groups stand behind two goal lines at the opposite ends of the activity area, facing each other. When the teacher gives a signal, both groups run forward toward the center. The net tries to catch as many fish as possible by making a circle around them by holding hands. The fish try to get out of the opening before the net closes. They cannot go through the net by going under the arms of the children, but if the net breaks because the children let go of each other's hands, the fish can go through the opening until the hands are joined again. The fish are safe if they get to the opposite goal line without being caught in the net. When the net has made its circle, the number of fish inside are counted and the score is recorded. The next time the groups change places.

Comment: The children get the *feel* of working together as a group with hands joined. They can see the need for keeping the net intact by holding hands firmly.

Join Hands Relay

Several relay teams form behind a starting line. The first member of each team stands on the opposite goal line, a given distance away, facing his relay team. At the signal to start, this first member runs to the second member of his team, takes him by the hand and together they run to the goal line. The first member remains there and the second member returns to bring back the third member. This procedure is continued until all members have reached the goal line. The winner is the first full team to arrive at the goal line.

Comment: It may be a good idea to arrange the children in such a way that they are nearly equal in running speed. That is, the purpose could be defeated if a very fast and a very slow runner were teamed up. The children must cooperate in running back to the goal line with hands joined, and thus they see and feel the importance of running together well for the success of the entire team.

Chain Tag

One child is chosen as leader. The leader chooses another child to assist him, and the two join hands. They chase the other children, trying to tag one. When a child has been tagged, he takes his place between the two and the chain grows. The first two, the leader and his assistant, remain at the ends throughout the activity, and are the only ones who can tag. When the chain surrounds a child, he may not break through the line or go under the hands. When the chain breaks, it must be reunited before tagging begins again. The game can end when the chain has five or more children. A new leader is chosen, and the game begins again.

Comment: In this game it is important for the children to keep a firm grasp of each other's hands, particularly as the chain grows. The children should discern the importance of this since the success of the activity depends upon it.

Cat and Mouse

One child is chosen to be the mouse and another child is the cat.

The remaining children join hands and form a circle, with the mouse in the center of the circle and the cat on the outside of the circle. The children in the circle try to keep the cat from getting into the circle and catching the mouse. If the cat gets inside the circle, the children in the circle let the mouse out of the circle and try to keep the cat in, but they must keep their hands joined at all times. When the cat catches the mouse the game is over and those players join the circle while two other children become the cat and mouse. If the mouse is not caught in a specified period of time, a new cat and mouse can be selected.

Comment: The children can see the importance of working together with joined hands. When the cat tries to enter the circle at a given point between two children, those two children can feel the right grip of the hands needed to protect the mouse.

Centipede Race

Children are arranged in teams and form rows. Each child reaches back between his legs with his right hand and grasps the left hand of the child immediately in back of him. On a signal, the joined-together teams race to the goal line some thirty to forty feet from the starting line and then race back to the starting line. The team finishing first with the line unbroken wins.

Comment: Each child should be sure to have a firm grip on the hand of the child behind him before the race starts. The children can see the importance of keeping the hands firmly joined to keep their teams intact.

Hook On

One child is selected as the runner. The remaining children form groups of four. The children in each of these groups of four stand one behind the other, each with his arms around the waist of the child in front. The runner attempts to hook on at the end of any group of four where he can. The group members twist and swing about, trying to protect their end from being caught. If the runner is successful, the leader of that group is the new runner. The group having the most of its original members at the end of a specified period of time is the winner.

Comment: The children need to exercise ingenuity as a group to protect the last person. Thus, the importance of being linked together as a group can be seen.

Rhythmic Activities

Most rhythmic activities involve tactile sensitivity, particularly those classified as singing games and dances. In these kinds of activities the entire group, or partners, move in various patterns with hands joined. In addition, various forms of body contact are involved in swinging a partner, clapping hands with a partner and the like. Some examples of these kinds of activities follow.

Charlie Over The Water

Verse
1. Charlie over the water.
2. Charlie over the sea.
3. Charlie caught a blackbird.
4. Can't catch me.

Action: One child is selected to be Charlie. The rest of the children form a circle and join hands. Charlie stands about two or three feet inside the circle. As the verse is sung, the children comprising the circle walk around counterclockwise while Charlie walks inside the circle clockwise. On the last word of the verse, all of the children stoop down. Charlie tries to tag the nearest child before he gets down. The activity continues with another child selected as Charlie.

Rabbit in the Hollow

Verse
1. Rabbit in the hollow sits and sleeps.
2. Hunter in the forest nearer creeps.
3. Little rabbit, have a care,

4. Deep within your hollow there.
5. Quickly to the forest,
6. You must run, run, run.

Action: The children form a circle with hands joined. One child, taking the part of the rabbit, crouches inside the circle while another child, taking the part of the hunter, stands outside the circle. A space nearby is designated as the rabbit's home, to which he may run and in which he is safe. On Lines 1 and 2 the children in the circle walk clockwise. On Lines 3 and 4, the children in the circle stand still and the rabbit tries to get away from the hunter by breaking through the circle and attempting to reach home without being tagged. If the rabbit is tagged, he chooses another child to be the rabbit. The hunter chooses another hunter.

Self-testing Activities

Many types of self-testing activities present excellent opportunities for experiences in tactile sensitivity. The classifications of self-testing activities considered here are apparatus activities, ball handling activities and stunt and tumbling activities.

The importance of *apparatus* activities for tactile experiences is seen as the child is given the opportunity to climb on various pieces of apparatus such as jungle gyms, climb-arounds and the like. Children get the feel of the use of the hands as the body is suspended from a horizontal bar or ladder as well as the feel of the texture in climbing a rope.

Several *ball handling* activities were described in Chapter 5, and these can be of value in tactile training. Many of the activities requiring control of a ball involve tactile discrimination.

Stunt activities provide fine possibilities for tactility in that many of them afford opportunities for body contact with other children as well as with the surface area. Some representative examples of these kinds of activities follow.

Seal Crawl

In the Seal Crawl, the child supports himself on his hands

while his body is extended back. The child squats, and places his hands shoulder width apart, palms flat and fingers pointed forward. He extends his legs in back of himself until his body is straight. The child points his toes so that a part of his weight will be on the top of his feet. He is now ready to move forward on his hands, dragging his feet.

Churn the Butter

Churn the Butter involves two children. These two turn back-to-back and lock elbows by bending their arms to approximately a ninety-degree angle. The elbows are held in back of each performer and the forearms are held against the ribs. One child picks up the other child from the surface area by bending forward with a slow, controlled movement. The other child will momentarily have his feet off the surface area. The first child releases the lifting force by straightening to an erect standing position; the other child then lifts the first child in the same manner. This action is repeated as long as desired. Children of nearly the same weight and strength should be paired for this stunt.

Wheelbarrow

Each child has a partner of about equal size and strength. One of the pair assumes a position with his hands on the surface area, his elbows straight, and his feet extended behind him. The other child carries the feet of the first child, who keeps his knees straight. He becomes a wheelbarrow by walking on his hands. Positions are changed so that each can become the wheelbarrow.

Tumbling activities such as the Log Roll, Forward Roll, and Backward Roll are useful for tactile sensitivity and have been described previously. In addition to these, the following are of value for the same purpose.

Side Roll

The child assumes the starting position by kneeling on the mat and placing his forehead on it as near his knees as possible. He then grasps his shins with his hands and pulls his feet from the mat. The objective is for the child to start the roll to either side, roll to the back, to the other side, and back to the knees and forehead position. The child should concentrate on rolling in a straight pattern along the mat.

Egg Roll

In the Egg Roll the child should roll from a sitting position to his side, to his back, to his other side, and back to the sitting position. The start is a sitting position on the mat with the knees close to the chest and the heels close to the buttocks. The child reaches inside his knees with his hands and grasps the outside of his shins. He is now ready to move to his side, in either direction, on his back, to his other side, and back to the sitting position.

Chapter 7

VISUAL AND AUDITORY PERCEPTION

THE visual and auditory systems provide two of the most important forms of sensory input for learning. The term *visual* is concerned with images that are obtained through the eyes. Thus, visual input involves the various learning media directed to the visual sense. The term *auditory* may be described as stimulation occurring through the sense organs of hearing. Therefore, auditory input is concerned with the various learning media directed to the auditory sense.

These two forms of sensory input complement each other in individuals who have both normal vision and hearing. However, as the extremes away from normalcy are approached — that is, in cases of complete or near-complete absence of one of the senses — their use as combined learning media obviously diminishes. However, at the extreme away from normalcy, a person relies a great deal upon the system which is functioning normally. For example, although the sightless person relies a great deal upon tactile perception, particularly as far as "reading" is concerned, he is also extremely sensitive to auditory input in the form of various sounds. In a like manner, the deaf person relies heavily upon the visual sense as a form of sensory input.

The relationship of these two senses in children with normal or near-normal functioning of both is seen in the area of reading. That is, there is a natural sequence from listening to reading, and the acquisition of the skill of auditory discrimination is an important factor in learning to read. Additionally, in many teaching-learning situations these two forms of sensory input are used in combination: for example, the teacher might use oral communication to describe something and display it at the same time. Of course, one of the important features for teachers to consider is the extent to which these aspects of sensory input should be used simultaneously. The teacher needs to be aware of how well children can handle the tasks together. In other words, if

107

visual and auditory input are combined in a teaching-learning situation, the teacher must determine whether or not, and to what extent, one becomes an attention-distracting factor for the other.

VISUAL PERCEPTION

Visual perception has been described as the mental interpretation of what a person sees.[1] A number of aspects of visual perception that have been identified include eye-motor coordination, figure-ground perception, form constancy, position in space, and spatial relationships. It has been suggested that children who show deficiency in these various areas may have difficulty in school performance. Various training programs have been devised to help correct or improve these conditions in children, with the idea that such training would result in the improvement of learning ability. The extent to which this has been accomplished has been extolled by some and seriously questioned by others. As indicated in Chapter 2, research involving this general type of training does not present clear-cut and definitive evidence to support the notion that such training results in academic achievement. Perhaps it should be pointed out again that compensatory physical education does *not* provide for structured training in its attempt to bring about improvement in learning ability. This is to say that the activities provided in this and other chapters of the text are those which are natural activities in the physical education experiences of children. And, although there is a lack of objective evidence to support the idea that participation in such activities brings about absolute improvement in learning ability, there nevertheless is abundant empirical support to justify children's participation in these activities.

ACTIVITIES INVOLVING VISUAL PERCEPTION

Before detailing some of the specific activities involving visual

---

[1]Donald C. Cushenbery and Kenneth J. Gilbreath, *Effective Reading Instruction for Slow Learners,* (Springfield, Illinois, Charles C Thomas Publisher, 1972): p. 98.

perception, it might be a good idea to discuss certain factors concerned with the *visual input phase* of a physical education lesson.

There are certain fundamental phases involved in almost every physical education teaching-learning situation. These phases are (1) auditory input (to be discussed later in the chapter), (2) visual input, (3) participation, and (4) evaluation.[2] Although some of these phases will be more important than others, they will occur in the teaching of practically every physical education lesson regardless of the type of activity being taught. While the application of the phases may be general in nature, they nevertheless should be utilized in such a way that they become specific in a particular situation. Depending upon the type of activity being taught — game, rhythm or self-testing activity — the use and application of the various phases should be characterized by flexibility and awareness of the objective of the lesson.

Various estimates indicate that the visual sense brings us upwards of three-fourths of our knowledge. If this postulation can be used as a valid criterion, the merits of the visual input phase in teaching physical education are readily discernible.

In general, there are two types of visual input which can be used satisfactorily in teaching physical education. These are visual symbols and human demonstration (live performance).

Visual Symbols

Included among the visual symbols used in physical education are motion pictures and various kinds of flat or still pictures. One of the disadvantages of the latter centers around the difficulty of portraying movement with a still figure. Although movement is shown in motion pictures, it is not depicted in the third dimension which causes some degree of ineffectiveness. One valuable use of visual symbols is that which employs diagrams to show dimensions of playing areas. This procedure may be useful when the teacher is explaining an activity in the classroom before moving to the outdoor activity area. Court dimensions and the

[2]James H. Humphrey, *Child Learning Through Elementary School Physical Education,* 2nd ed. (Dubuque, Iowa, Wm. C. Brown Publisher, 1974): p. 70.

like can be diagrammed on the chalkboard, providing a good opportunity for integration with other areas such as mathematics and drawing to scale.

Human Demonstration

Some of the guides to action in the use of demonstration follow.

1. If the teacher plans to demonstrate, this should be included in preparation of the lesson by practicing and rehearsing the demonstration.

2. The teacher does not need to do all of the demonstrating — in fact, in some cases it may be much more effective to have one or more pupils demonstrate. Since the teacher is expected to be a skilled performer, a demonstration by a pupil will oftentimes serve to show other children that one of their own classmates can perform the activity and that they might also be able to do it. In addition, it may be entirely possible that the teacher may not be an efficient enough performer to demonstrate a certain activity. For example, it may be necessary for some teachers to call upon pupils to demonstrate some of the more complex stunt and tumbling activities.

3. If the teacher prefers to do the demonstrating in a given situation, it still may be advisable to use pupils to demonstrate in order to show the class that the performance of the activity is within its realm of achievement.

4. The demonstration should be based upon the skill and ability of a given group of children. If it appears to be too difficult for them, they may not want to attempt the activity.

5. When at all possible, a demonstration should parallel the timing and conditions of the game or activity. However, if the situation is one in which the movements are complex or done with great speed, it might be a good idea to have the demonstration conducted at a slower pace than that involved in the actual playing or performance.

6. The group should be arranged so everyone is in a favorable position to see the demonstration. Moreover, the children should be able to view the demonstration from a position in which it takes place. For example, if the activity is to be

performed in a lateral plane, children should be placed so that they can see it from this position.

7. Although demonstration and auditory input can be satisfactorily combined in many situations, as mentioned previously, care should be taken that an explanation is not lost because the visual sense offsets the auditory sense. That is, one sense should not become an attention-distracting factor for the other.

8. After the demonstration has been presented, it may be a good practice to demonstrate again and to have the children go through the movements with the demonstrator. This allows the use of both the kinesthetic sense and the visual sense, closely integrating these two sensory stimuli.

9. Demonstrations should not be too long. Children are eager to participate, and this opportunity should be provided as soon as possible after the demonstration.

The activities which follow are primarily concerned with *visualization* and *visual-motor coordination*. Visualization involves visual image, which is the mental reconstruction of a visual experience, or the result of mentally combining a number of visual experiences.[3] Visual-motor coordination is concerned with visual-motor tasks that involve the integration of vision and movement.

Game Activities

Jump the Shot

The children form a circle with one child, standing in its center, holding a length of rope with an object tied to one end. The object should be something soft, such as a beanbag. The player in the center of the circle starts the game by swinging the object on the rope around and around close to the feet of the players in the circle. The players in the circle attempt to avoid being hit by the object by jumping over it when it goes by them. A point can be

---

[3]Carter V. Good, *Dictionary of Education,* 2nd ed. (New York, McGraw-Hill, Inc., 1959): p. 279.

scored against any person hit on the feet by the object on the rope.

Comment: This activity provides a good opportunity for visual-motor coordination as a child must quickly coordinate his movement with the visual experience. This can be a good evaluative technique for the teacher since he can see how well the child makes the judgments necessary to jump over the object at the proper time.

Ball Pass

The players are divided into two or more groups and each group forms a circle. The object of the game is to pass the ball around the circle to see who can get it around first. The teacher gives the directions for the ball to be passed or tossed from one player to another. For example, the teacher may say, "Pass the ball to the right, toss the ball over two players," and so on. The game may be varied by using more than one ball of different sizes and weights. For instance, a basketball, volleyball, and tennis ball might be used.

Comment: This activity provides a good opportunity to improve eye-hand coordination, and it has been observed that after practice in this activity poor coordination can be improved.

Policeman

One child is selected to be the policeman, and sides are chosen. The groups stand equidistant from the policeman. The policeman carries a card, red on one side and green on the other. At the signal to go (green) from the policeman, each group sees how far it can get before the stop signal (red) is given. Any child who moves after the *stop* signal is given must go back to the original starting point. When all members of a side have passed the policeman, that group is declared the winner.

Comment: Rather than using the colors, the words *Stop* and *Go* can be used so that the children can become familiar with the words as well as the colors. This activity helps children coordinate movement with the visual experience. This game can help children become more adept at visual-motor association. The teacher should be alert to observe those children who do not stop on signal, as well as those who look to others for clues.

Keep It Up

Depending upon the ability level of the children, a large rubber playground ball, a beach ball, or even a large balloon can be used for this activity. Children are divided into several small circles, with each circle having a ball. On a signal, one child tosses the ball into the air and the other children try to see how long they can keep the ball up without letting it touch the surface area. The group that keeps it in the air for the longer time is the winner.

Comment: This is a good activity for the improvement of eye-hand coordination.

Figure Relay

Two lines are drawn about thirty feet apart on the activity area. The group is divided into two teams. Both teams stand behind one of the lines. The teacher displays the form of a geometric figure cut out of cardboard. The teams run across to the opposite line and form the figure. The team that forms the figure correctly first wins a point. The teams then line up behind that line, and when the teacher displays another figure, they run to the opposite line and again form the figure the teacher has displayed. The geometric figures should be those that the children have been working with such as the circle, square, rectangle and triangle.

Comment: This activity can be useful in improving form perception. It helps children to work together to produce a given form which is displayed by the teacher. It has been observed that children who have problems with figure-ground relationships may also have difficulty with form perception. Thus, this activity can be of value to those children who have problems in both figure-ground relationships and form perception.

The importance of visual perception in *reading* is obvious; moreover, it has been demonstrated that active games can play an important part in the aspects of visual perception pertaining to *visual discrimination* and *sight vocabulary*. Visual discrimination is the ability to distinguish one object from another, and sight vocabulary is concerned with those words that the child immediately recognizes as he reads without having to resort to word-analysis techniques. The remainder of this section of the chapter is devoted to representative examples of games which can be utilized specifically for these two purposes. The following games are directed to the improvement of visual discrimination.

Match Cats

For as many children as are in the class, the teacher makes duplicate sets of cards with pictures or designs on them. The cards are passed out randomly. On a signal, or as the music starts, the children move around the activity area with a specified locomotor movement such as hopping or skipping. When the music stops, or a signal is given, each child finds the person with his duplicate card, joins one hand, and they sit down together. The last couple down become the Match Cats for that turn. The children then get up and exchange cards. The game continues in the same manner with different locomotor movements used.

Comment: Depending upon the level of skills development of the children, the cards may be pictures of real objects or abstract forms, colors, alphabet letters, and words.

Mother May I

The children stand in a line at one end of the activity area. The teacher has cards showing object pairs, similar and different. The teacher holds up one pair of the cards. If the paired objects or symbols are the same, the children may take one giant step forward. Any child who moves when he sees an unpaired set of cards must return to the starting line. The object of the game is to reach the finish line on the opposite side of the activity area.

Comment: The teacher may select cards to test any level of visual discrimination. Using pairs of cards for categorizing pictures would utilize concept and language development.

Match Cards

Each child in the group is given a colored card, with several children receiving duplicate cards. There are two chairs placed in the center of the activity area. On a signal, the children may walk, skip, hop, etc., to music around the activity area. When the music stops, the teacher holds up a card. Those children whose cards match the teacher's card run to sit in the chairs. Anyone getting a seat scores a point, and play resumes. Cards should be exchanged frequently among the children.

Comment: This visual discrimination activity can be adapted easily to include increasingly complex visual discrimination tasks. Scoring points could be made more difficult by changing the movements necessary to score points. Visual discrimination tasks might also include shapes, designs, and letters (both capital and lower case).

The following are some representative games involving sight vocabulary. There is a great deal of empirical support for the use of active games in helping children gain mastery in sight vocabulary. Recently, a study by Dickerson[4] provided some objective evidence for this theoretical postulation. The study showed that first grade children learn sight vocabulary words significantly better through active games than with passive (sedentary) games and traditional procedures.

More specifically, the following results were obtained.

1. Girls in the active games group achieved significantly higher scores than girls in the passive games group.
2. Boys in the active games group achieved significantly higher scores than boys in the passive games group.
3. Within the groups there were no statistically significant differences in achievement between girls and boys.

Call Phrase

The children form a circle facing the center. One child is designated as the caller and stands in the center of the circle. Each

---

[4]Dolores Pawley Dickerson, "A Comparison of the Use of the Active Game Learning Medium with Passive Games and Traditional Activities as a Means of Reinforcing Recognition of Selected Sight Vocabulary Words with Mid-year First Grade Children with Limited Sight Vocabularies." Doctoral Dissertation, University of Maryland, College Park, Maryland, 1975.

child is given a card with a phrase printed on it. Several children can have the same phrase. The caller draws a card from a box containing corresponding phrase cards and holds up the card for everyone to see. Reading the phrase is the signal for those children in the circle with the same phrase to exchange places before the caller can fill in one of the vacant places in the circle. The remaining child can become the caller. If the child in the center cannot read the phrase, he can get help from the teacher or another child.

Comment: Children need opportunities to develop quick recognition of phrases. This game provides the repetition necessary to help children develop familiarity with phrases they are meeting in their reading material. The phrases may be taken from group experience stories, readers, or children's own experience stories.

Word Erase

The children are divided into several teams. The teams form rows at a specified distance from a chalkboard. Previously the teacher has written lists of words from the children's experience stories and readers, one list for each team. On a signal the first child on each team calls the first word. If he is correct, as determined by the teacher, he runs to the board and erases it, then returns to the rear of his team. If he does not know the word, he may ask for help from one member of his team. The second child continues in the same manner. The game is won by the first team finished.

Comment: Words selected for this game may come from experience stories and stories read on that or the previous day. This game provides necessary repetition to develop instant recognition of words and can be used to maintain words.

Word Carpet

Several forms such as squares, circles or triangles are drawn on the floor, or pieces of paper in the shape of these forms are placed on the floor to represent magic carpets. Each magic carpet is numbered from one to three to correspond with a numbered list of words on the chalkboard. The words include new vocabulary from the children's experience; stories, readers, and social studies and science units. Two teams of children are selected, and each team forms a chain by holding hands. To music, the two teams walk around in circles and back and forth in a zig-zag manner over the magic carpets until the music stops. Each child then standing on or closest to the magic carpet identifies any word from the numbers list on the board that corresponds with the number at that magic carpet. If it is read correctly, the teacher erases that word from the list. Each team scores one point for any correctly identified word. The team with the highest score wins.

Comment: This game provides an interesting activity, to give new words additional emphasis. To focus on the meaning of new words, the teacher can require the child who has read a word correctly to put it in a sentence. If he accomplishes the task, the team will score an additional point. Children can also be helped to identify specific word analysis clues they used to identify their words.

Rhythmic Activities

Many of the singing games and dances can provide opportunities for training in figure-ground relationships and improvement in form perception. In addition to the development of forms in certain dance patterns, the different formations for dances such as line, circle and square are useful experiences for children.

Numerous dances provide for eye-hand and eye-foot coordination and, as such, are valuable experiences in developing those forms of visual perception. A specific example is the dance *Children's Polka* described in Chapter 5.

Self-testing Activities

Many outstanding opportunities for experiences in visual

perception are inherent in self-testing activities. Those presented here will focus upon the aspects of visual perception concerned with eye-hand coordination, eye-foot coordination and figure-ground relationships. The classifications of self-testing activities used here for this purpose are *skills of propulsion and retrieval, ball handling activities,* and *balance beam activities.*

Skills of Propulsion and Retrieval

Included among the skills of propulsion and retrieval are the following:

1. *Throwing* — Release of an object with one or both hands.
2. *Striking* — Propelling an object with a part of the body (such as the hand) or an implement (such as a bat).
3. *Kicking* — Propelling an object with either foot.
4. *Catching* — Retrieving an object with the hands or arms.
5. *Trapping* — Stopping an object with the feet.

The skills in this classification considered here for use in visual perception are throwing, kicking and catching. Ordinarily, the object to be propelled or retrieved will be a ball, and in some instances, a beanbag. Hereafter in this discussion the object will be referred to as "the ball."

THROWING. As mentioned above, the skill of throwing involves the release of a ball with one or both hands. In general, there are three factors involved in successful throwing. These are the accuracy or direction of the throw, the distance which a ball must be thrown, and the amount of force needed to propel the ball.

Any release of an object from the hand or hands could be considered as an act of throwing. Thought of in these terms, the average infant of six months is able to perform a reasonable facsimile of throwing from a sitting position. It has been estimated that, by four years of age, about twenty percent of the children show at least a degree of proficiency in throwing. This ability tends to increase rapidly, and between the ages of five and six, over three-fourths of the children have attained a reasonable degree of proficiency as previously defined here.

In the early throwing behavior of children, boys tend to perform better than girls. At all age levels, boys are generally superior to girls in throwing for distance. There is not such a pronounced sex difference evident in throwing for accuracy, although the performance of boys in this aspect tends to exceed that of girls.

There are three generally accepted throwing *patterns*. These are the (1) underarm pattern, (2) sidearm pattern, and (3) overarm pattern. It should be noted that although the ball is released by one or both hands, the term "arm" is used in connection with the various patterns. The reason for this is that the patterns involve a "swing" of the arm.

The child ordinarily begins the *underarm throwing pattern* by releasing the ball from both hands. However, he is soon able to release with one hand, especially when the ball is small enough for him to grip.

At the starting position, the thrower stands facing the direction of the throw. The feet should be in a parallel position and slightly apart. The right arm* is in a position nearly perpendicular to the surface area. To start the throw, the right arm is brought back (back swing) to a position where it is about parallel with the surface area. Simultaneously, there is a slight rotation of the body to the right with most of the weight transferred to the right foot. As the arm comes forward (front swing), a step is taken with the left foot. (Stepping out with the opposite foot of the swinging arm is known as the *principle of opposition*.) The ball is released on the front swing when the arm is about parallel to the surface area. During the process of the arm swing, the arm is straight, describing a semicircle with no flexion at the elbow. The right foot is carried forward as a part of the follow-through after the release.

In the *side arm throwing pattern*, aside from the direction the thrower faces and the plane of the arm swing, the mechanical principles applied are essentially the same as for the underarm throwing pattern.

The thrower faces at a right angle to the direction of the throw, whereas in the underarm throwing pattern he faces in the direction of the throw. The arm is brought to the back swing in a horizontal plane, or a position parallel to the surface area. Body rotation and weight shift is the same as in the underarm pattern. The arm remains straight and a semicircle is described from the backswing to the release of the ball on the front swing.

---

*All of the descriptions involving the skills of propulsion and retrieval are for a right-handed child. In the case of the left-handed child, just the opposite should apply.

The sidearm throwing pattern will ordinarily be used to propel a ball that is too large to grip with one hand. Thus, on the backswing, the opposite hand helps control the ball until there is sufficient momentum during the swing. Greater distance can be obtained with the sidearm throwing pattern with a ball too large to grip, but accuracy is more difficult to achieve.

In the *overarm throwing pattern,* the basic mechanics are essentially the same as for the two previous patterns. The thrower faces in a direction somewhere between that used in the two previous patterns. This position is likely to vary from one individual to another and should not be standardized as a fixed position. An essential difference in the overarm throwing pattern is in the position of the arm. Whereas in the two previous patterns the arm was kept straight, in the overarm throwing pattern there is flexion at the elbow. Thus, on the backswing the arm is brought back with the elbow bent, and with the arm at a right angle away from the body. The arm is then brought forward and the ball is released with a "whiplike" motion at about the height of the shoulder. Foot and arm follow through is the same as with the underarm and sidearm throwing patterns. This pattern is used for throwing a ball that can be gripped with the fingers when distance as well as accuracy is important.

All of these patterns can be used to develop eye-hand coordination. This can be done by using either balls of different sizes or beanbags to throw at a target. The stationary targets can be of different shapes and sizes, and a teacher is limited only by his or her imagination in this regard. The type of throwing pattern used, as well as the distance, will depend upon the skill and ability level of the child. One authority stresses that when presenting young children with target tasks (that is, throwing at a wall target), teachers should provide objects large enough to be clearly seen; and, furthermore, that when children work with relatively small target objects, the best visual input occurs at a distance of no less than six feet from the object.[5]

---

[5]Hope M. Smith, "Implications for Movement Education Experiences Drawn from Perceptual-Motor Research," *Journal of Health, Physical Education and Recreation,* April 1970.

KICKING. As early as age two the average child is able to maintain his balance on one foot and propel a stationary ball with the other foot. At this early stage the child is likely to have limited action of the kicking foot with little or no follow through. With advancing age, better balance is maintained with greater increments of strength, and by age six the child can develop a full leg backswing and a body lean into the kick with a stationary ball.

In kicking, contact with the ball is made with the (1) inside of the foot, (2) outside of the foot, or (3) instep of the foot. With the exception of these positions of the foot, the mechanical principles of kicking are essentially the same. The kicking leg is swung back with flexion at the knee. The leg swings forward with the foot making contact with the ball. Contact can be made when the ball is either stationary or moving.

There is not complete agreement in terms of progression in the skill of kicking. My personal preference of sequence follows.

1. *Stationary.* The ball and the kicker remain stationary. That is, the kicker stands beside the ball and kicks it. The kicker is concerned only with the leg movement and it is more likely that he will keep his head down with his eyes on the ball at the point of contact.

2. *Stationary and run.* This means that the ball is in a stationary position and that the kicker takes a short run up to the ball before kicking it. This is more difficult since the kicker must time and coordinate his run to make proper contact with the ball.

3. *Kick from hands.* This is referred to as "punting," as in football and soccer. The kicker drops the ball from his hands, takes one or two steps, then kicks the ball as it drops. He is kicking a moving target but he has control over the movement of the ball before kicking it.

4. *Kicking from a pitcher.* This means that another person pitches or rolls the ball to the kicker, as in the game of kickball. This is perhaps the most difficult kick because the kicker must kick a moving ball that is under the control of another person.

Various kinds of kicking experiences can be important to the improvement of eye-foot coordination. Children can begin by just kicking a ball with either foot. Different sized balls can be used, and in some instances, as for beginners, it may be a good idea to use a beachball. After children are able to kick the ball with either foot, they can alternate feet. This is accomplished by running along with the ball, and is known as *foot dribbling*. It can be a good experience to have children try to kick the ball at a stationary target, using different sized balls and targets at varying distances. When children become proficient at hitting a stationary target with the ball, they can attempt to kick at a moving target. One way of doing this is for the teacher to roll a ball and have the children try to hit it by kicking another ball at it.

CATCHING. Catching with the hands is the most frequently used retrieving skill, although as mentioned previously, a ball can be retrieved with the feet, as in "trapping" the ball in the game of soccer.

One of the child's first experiences in catching occurs at an early stage in life when he sits with his legs in a spread position and another person rolls a ball to him. By four years of age about one-third of the children can retrieve a ball in aerial flight thrown from a short distance. Slightly over half of them can perform this feat by age five, and about two-thirds of them can accomplish this by age six.

Generally speaking, it has been observed that children achieve the same skill level sooner in catching with a larger ball than they do with a smaller ball. The reason for this may lie in the way the child tries to catch the ball, as suggested in a study by Victors.[6] She selected twenty boys for inclusion in a cinematography study. On the basis of a predetermined catching performance score and the subjective ranking of the physical education teacher, the five most successful and the five least successful boys were selected from each level. Each child was filmed during four consecutive catching attempts, two with a three-inch ball and two with a ten-inch ball. It was found that ball size did not generally determine success or failure in catching. The size of the ball, however, did make a difference in the type of catch utilized by the children. The

---

[6]Evelyn Victors, "A Cinematography Study of the Catching Behavior of Selected Nine and Ten-year-old Boys," Doctoral Dissertation, University of Wisconsin, Madison, Wisconsin, 1968.

arms and body were used more frequently with the larger ball, resulting in a "basket catch." There was evidence of more hand closure success with the smaller ball.

Studies have been conducted in an attempt to determine effects of velocity, projective angle, and time of ball in flight. One such study by Bruce[7] using second, fourth and sixth grade boys and girls indicated that catching performance improved with grade level; that boys were superior to girls in catching performance; that younger, lesser skilled children showed poorer performance as ball velocity increased; and that changes in vertical angle of projection had little effect on catching performance. It was further indicated that variation in time of ball flight had no significant effect on catching performance.

There are certain basic mechanical principles that should be taken into account in the skill of catching. It is of utmost importance that the catcher position himself as nearly "in line" with the ball as possible. In this position he will be better able to receive the ball near the body's center of gravity. Another important factor is hand position. A ball will approach the catcher (1) at the waist, (2) above the waist, or (3) below the waist. When the ball approaches at about waist level, the palms should be facing each other with fingers pointing straight ahead. The "heels" of the hands should be close together depending upon the size of the ball. That is, closer together for a small ball and farther apart for a large ball. When the ball approaches above the waist the palms face the ball and the fingers point upward with the thumbs as close together as necessary. When the ball approaches below the waist, the palms still face the ball but the fingers point downward with the little fingers as close together as seems necessary, depending again upon the size of the ball. When the ball reaches the hands, it is brought in toward the body. That is, the catcher "gives" with the catch in order to control the ball and absorb the shock. It is likely that the position of the feet will depend upon the speed with which the ball approaches. Ordinarily, one foot should be in advance of the other in a stride position, with the distance

---

[7]Russel D. Bruce, "The Effects of Variations in Ball Trajectory upon the Catching Performance of Elementary School Children," Doctoral Dissertation, University of Wisconsin, Madison, Wisconsin, 1966.

determined by the speed of the approaching ball.

Over a period of years there has been a controversy over whether or not a person should keep his eye on the ball when retrieving it. Whiting[8], who has done a considerable amount of study in this area, generalizes that it is important to encourage beginners in any ball skill to keep their eyes on the ball. On the other hand, he also indicates that although the beginner needs to watch the ball for as long as possible in order to take in the necessary visual information which will determine his actions, the expert is able to utilize information which comes at an early stage in ball flight. And further, the expert will not only need to watch the ball for less of its flight, but he will also require less time to discriminate, program and make decisions on the information that he receives about position of the ball, direction and force of wind, state of the ground, position of other players, and the many other cues in the display during any game situation. Smith[9] makes the important point that the speed of objects thrown or propelled toward the child should be minimal to allow for gradual focal convergence.

Useful catching skills for improvement of eye-hand coordination include catching various kinds of objects thrown against and rebounding from a wall, catching objects thrown by the teacher or another child, and catching objects propelled into the air and retrieved by the individual himself.

Ball Handling Activities

The various kinds of ball handling activities provide outstanding experiences for eye-hand coordination. The activities that follow have been described elsewhere in the text for use in other frames of reference. They are described again here for purposes of continuity and convenience.

STATIONARY BOUNCE. Using both hands, bounce a ball to the surface area and catch it while standing in place. This can be repeated any number of times.

---

[8]H. T. A. Whiting, *Acquiring Ball Skills* (Philadelphia, Lea & Febiger, 1969): p. 34-35.
[9]Hope M. Smith, "Implications for Movement Education Experiences Drawn from Perceptual-Motor Research," *Journal of Health, Physical Education and Recreation,* April, 1970.

WALKING BOUNCE. Using both hands, bounce the ball to the surface area and catch it while walking.

PARTNER BOUNCE. Using both hands, bounce the ball to a partner who returns it. The distance between the partners can be increased as desired.

BOUNCE AROUND. Children form a circle. The first child, using both hands, bounces the ball to the child next to him, who retrieves it and bounces it to the next. The circle can be made up of any number of children; however, not more than five are recommended so that children will get the greatest number of turns.

STATIONARY TAP. The child taps the ball with one hand while standing in place. Either hand can be used depending upon the individual child, and the tapping can be repeated any number of times.

WALKING TAP. Tap the ball while walking along. This can be done any number of times.

THROW AND CATCH. Throw the ball into the air and catch it. The height of the throw can be increased as desired.

BOUNCE-CLAP-CATCH. Bounce the ball to the surface area and clap the hands before catching it.

BOUNCE-TURN-CATCH. Bounce the ball and turn around to catch it before it bounces a second time. At the outset of this activity it may be a good idea to throw the ball into the air and then turn around to catch it on the bounce. In the variation the child has more time to turn around before the ball bounces.

LEG-OVER BOUNCE. Bounce the ball, swing the leg over it, and catch it. This can be done with either leg, and then legs can be alternated.

LEG-OVER TAP. This is the same as the Leg-over Bounce except that the child causes the ball to bounce by continuous tapping.

Balance Beam Activities

Activities on the balance beam provide many good opportunities for perceptual-motor training; here we will be concerned with those activities which can develop children's ability to discern figure-ground relationships. According to Morris and Whiting[10]

---

[10]P. R. Morris and H. T. A. Whiting, *Motor Impairment and Compensatory Education* (Philadelphia, Lea & Febiger, 1971): p. 217.

training in figure-ground perception "is aimed at improving a child's ability to select and focus his attention upon the relevant stimuli in his visual field and to ignore the irrelevant stimuli. In addition, it is also intended to increase the efficiency with which a child scans the display and his ability to shift his attention as the situation changes." These same authors also assert that "by working for short periods within a clearly structured routine, a child may be encouraged to direct more of his attention to the stimuli that are relevant to the task at hand." It is this kind of situation which the following balance beam activities provide. As in the case of the preceding ball handling activities, the balance beam activities suggested here have been described before and are repeated again for purposes of convenience and continuity. Also, procedures for teaching balance beam activities were given in Chapter 5 and perhaps should be reviewed by the reader.

FRONT WALK. Walk forward on the beam using any length of step.

FRONT AND BACK WALK. Walk forward to the center of the beam using any length of step; turn and continue, walking backward to the end of the beam, using any length of step.

FORWARD FRONT WALK. Walk forward on the beam with either foot always in front of the other. The lead foot moves forward and the trailing foot comes up to the lead foot but not beyond.

FRONT WALK RETRIEVE OBJECT. Place an object such as a chalkboard eraser or a book in the center of the beam. Walk forward, stoop down and pick up the object, rise, and walk to the end of the beam before dismounting.

FRONT WALK OBJECT BALANCE. Place an object on the head. Mount the beam and walk the length of the beam while balancing the object on the head.

FRONT WALK OVER. Have two children hold a piece of string or rope stretched across the center of the beam at a height of about twelve to fifteen inches. Walk forward on the beam, step over the string and continue walking to the end of the beam.

FRONT WALK UNDER. Have two children hold a piece of string or rope stretched across the center of the beam at a height of from three to four feet. Walk forward on the beam, stoop down, move under the string, then stand and walk to the end of the beam.

AUDITORY PERCEPTION

It was estimated several years ago that about seventy-five percent of the waking hours is spent in verbal communication — forty-five percent in listening, thirty percent in speaking, sixteen percent in reading, and the remaining nine percent in writing.[11] If this estimate can be used as a valid criterion, the importance of developing skills of listening cannot be denied. If children are going to learn to listen effectively, care should be taken to improve upon their auditory perception — the mental interpretation of what a person hears.[12]

It will be the purpose of the remainder of this chapter to identify activities which can help to improve the factors necessary for auditory perception.

ACTIVITIES INVOLVING AUDITORY PERCEPTION

Before getting into some of the specific activities involving auditory perception, it might be a good idea to discuss certain factors concerned with the *auditory input phase* of a physical education lesson. In this connection, the factors taken into account are (1) preparing the children for listening, (2) teacher-pupil and pupil-pupil interaction, and (3) directionality of sound.

Preparing the Children for Listening

Since it is likely that the initial part of the auditory-input phase will originate with the teacher, care should be taken to prepare the children for listening. The teacher may set the scene by relating the activity to the interests of the children. In addition, the teacher should be on the alert to help children develop their own reasons

---

[11]George D. Spache, *Toward Better Reading* (Champaign, Illinois, Garrard Publishing Company, 1963): p. 181.

[12]Donald C. Cushenbery and Kenneth J. Gilbreath, *Effective Reading Instruction for Slow Learners* (Springfield, Illinois, Charles C Thomas Publisher, 1972): p. 98.

for listening.

In preparing children to listen, the teacher should be aware that it is of extreme importance to take into consideration the comfort of the children, and that attempts should be made to alleviate any possible distractions. Although evidence concerning the effect of environmental distraction on listening effectiveness is in short supply, there is reason to believe that distraction does interfere with listening comprehension. Moreover, it was reported a good many years ago that being able to see, as well as hear the speaker, is an important factor in listening distraction.[13]

All of these factors have a variety of implications for the auditory input phase of the physical education teaching-learning situation. For example, consideration should be given to the placement of pupils when a physical education activity is being explained to them. This means, for instance, that if the teacher is providing auditory input from a circle formation, he should take a position as part of the circle instead of speaking from the center of the circle. Moreover, if the group is large, perhaps it would be best to place the children in a small group for the auditory input phase and then put them into formation for the activity. Also it might be wise for teachers to consider that an object, such as a ball, could become a distraction when an activity is being explained. The attention of children is sometimes focused on the ball, and they may not listen to what is being said. The teacher might wish to conceal such an object until time for its use is most appropriate.

Teacher-pupil and Pupil-pupil Interaction

Since the auditory input phase of physical education is a two-way process, it is important to take into account certain factors involving verbal interaction of pupils with pupils and pupils with teacher.

By "democracy" some people seem to mean everyone doing or saying whatever happens to cross his mind at the moment; and

---

[13]Edward J. Kramer and Thomas R. Lewis, "Comparison of Visual and Nonvisual Listening," *Journal of Communication*, November 1951.

this raises the question of control. It should be emphasized that *group discussions*, if they are to be democratic, and if they are to be productive, must be under control. In brief, disciplined, controlled group discussion can be a training ground for living in a society in which both individual and group interests are profoundly respected.

Another important function in teacher-pupil verbal interaction is that concerned with time given to questions after the teacher has given an explanation. The teacher should give time for questions from the group, but should be very skillful in the use of questions. It must be determined immediately whether or not a question is a legitimate one. This implies that the type of questions asked can help to serve as criteria for the teacher to evaluate the auditory input phase of teaching. For example, if numerous questions are asked, it is apparent that either the auditory input from the teacher was incomplete or the children were not paying attention.

Directionality of Sound

In summarizing recent findings concerned with the directionality of sound, Smith has pointed up a number of interesting factors which are important to the auditory input phase.[14] She mentions that individuals tend to initiate movement toward the direction from which the sound cue emanates. For example, if a given verbal cue instructs an individual to move a body segment or segments to the left, but emanates from the right side of the individual, the initial motor response is to the right, followed by a reverse response to the left. Emphasizing the importance of this at the elementary school level, Smith recommends that when working on direction of motor responses with young children, one should make certain that sound cues come from the direction in which the motor response is to be made. The point stressed is that children have enough difficulty discriminating left from right without further confounding them.

---

[14]Hope M. Smith, "Implications for Movement Education Experiences Drawn from Perceptual-Motor Research," *Journal of Health, Physical Education and Recreation*, April, 1970.

Game Activities

Do This Do That

The children stand in a line and a child, selected as the leader, stands in front of the group and says, "Do this." At the same time he makes some sort of movement, such as swinging his arms, running in place, or the like. The players try to follow and keep up with what the leader is doing. The leader may say "Do that" and continue to make a movement. However, the players are not supposed to follow the movement when the leader says "Do that." A point can be scored against any player caught.

Comment: The players stand in a line rather than in a circle so that they all get the same view of the leader. This activity can give children practice in auditory and visual association as they listen for the cues and determine whether or not to perform the movement. There is also an opportunity for the development of *auditory image* which is the mental reconstruction of a hearing experience, or the mental combination of separate hearing experiences.[15]

I Say Stoop

The teacher or a child acting as the leader stands in front of the group which has formed a line. The leader says either, "I say stoop" or "I say stand." The leader carries out actions, but the class must carry out the commands rather than his actions. For example, if he says "I say stand" and he stoops all of the children who failed to follow the command, but follow the action, would have a point scored against them. Many opposite action or direction words could be used, such as: in and out, stop and go, run and walk, up and down, forward and backward, etc. If the leader cannot think of two words, or if there are specific words that need attention, the teacher can whisper those words to the leader.

---

[15]Carter V. Good, *Dictionary of Education*, 2nd ed. (New York, McGraw-Hill, Inc., 1959): p. 279.

Comment: This activity not only provides for alertness in auditory-motor association, but also can give practice in recognizing word opposites.

Boiling Water

Two or more circles are formed. Each circle is given one or more balls. A container such as a wastebasket is set along the sidelines of the activity area. One child in each circle is the leader. When the teacher calls "cold water," the children in each circle *pass* the ball from one child to the next. Whenever the teacher calls "warm water," the children *roll* the ball across the center of the circle from one to another. If the teacher calls "boiling water," the children throw the ball to different ones in the circle. When the teacher calls "water vapor," the ball is immediately thrown to the circle leader who then runs with it to the container on the sidelines. The team whose leader reaches the container first wins.

Comment: This game can be used as a diagnostic technique to help determine how well children can discern auditory cues and perform the action required.

Stoop Tag

The children form a circle and join hands. One child is *It* and stands in the center of the circle. The children walk around the circle saying:

> I am happy! I am free!
> I am down! You can't catch me!

At the word "down" the children stoop and let go of each other's hands. Then they stand up and jump and hop about, daring the child who is *It* to tag them. They must stoop to avoid being tagged. If a child is tagged when he is not stooping, he becomes *It*.

Comment: The child first learns to act on the basis of verbal instructions by others. In this regard it has been suggested that later he learns to guide and direct his own behavior on the basis of his own language activities — he literally talks to himself, giving

himself instructions.[16] This point of view is supported by research, particularly that of Luria,[17] who has postulated that
speech as a form of communication between children and adults
later becomes a means of organizing the child's own behavior.
That is, the function which was previously divided between two
people — child and adult — later becomes a function of human
behavior. The point in this activity is that the child tells himself
what to do and then does it: He says "I am down," then carries out
this action.

Dog Chase

The class is divided into five or six groups. The members of
each group are given the name of a dog, such as collie, poodle, and
so on. The small groups then mingle into one large group. One
child, acting as the leader, throws a ball or other object away from
the groups, at the same time calling out one of the dog names. All
of the children with this dog name run after the object. The one
who gets possession of it first becomes the leader for the next time.

Comment: The teacher can use this activity as a diagnostic
technique by observing those children who react slowly or do not
react at all to the auditory input.

Reading specialists are becoming more and more aware of the
importance of auditory perception as one of the early steps in
learning to read. It is suggested by some that the ability to discriminate sounds auditorily is not only an advantage in speech but
probably gives an important boost to reading learning ability.[18] It
has been found that active games can play an important part in
the aspect of auditory perception that is concerned with auditory
discrimination.[19] The remainder of this section of the chapter is

[16]S. Glucksberg, *Symbolic Processes* (Dubuque, Iowa, Wm. C. Brown Company
Publishers, 1966).
[17]A. R. Luria, Development of the Directive Function of Speech in Early Childhood,
Word, 1959.
[18]Donald C. Cushenbery and Kenneth J. Gilbreath, *Effective Reading Instruction for Slow
Learners* (Springfield, Illinois, Charles C Thomas Publisher, 1972): p. 36.
[19]James H. Humphrey and Dorothy D. Sullivan, *Teaching Slow Learners Through Active
Games* (Springfield, Illinois, Charles C Thomas Publisher, 1970): p. 59-64.

devoted to some representative examples of games which can be utilized specifically for use in auditory discrimination.

Man from Mars

One child is selected to be the Man from Mars and stands in the center of the activity area. The other children stand behind a designated line at one end of the activity area. The game begins when the children call out "Man from Mars, can we chase him through the stars?" The teacher answers, "Yes, if your name begins like duck" (or any other word). All of the children whose names begin with the same beginning sound as *duck* (or whatever word is called), chase the Man from Mars until he is caught. The child who tags him becomes the new Man from Mars, and the game continues.

Comment: In order for the children to run at the right time, they must listen carefully and match beginning sounds. Individual help can be given those children the teacher observes not running when they should. Children can also listen for words beginning like or ending like other words the teacher may use for the key word.

Mouse and Cheese

A round mousetrap is formed by the children standing in a circle. In the center of the mousetrap is placed the cheese (a ball, or some other object). The children are then assigned consonant digraphs *sh, ch, th*. Several children will have the same consonant digraph. That is, if there are thirty children, three will have the same consonant digraph. When the teacher calls a word beginning with a consonant digraph, all of the children with this digraph run around the circle and back to their original place, representing the hole in the trap. Through these original places they run into the circle to get the cheese. The child who gets the cheese is the winning mouse. Another word is called, and the same procedure is followed. Children may be assigned different digraphs from time to time.

Comment: Children need repetition in order to develop the ability to hear and identify various sound elements within words. This game enables children to recognize consonant digraphs within the context of whole words. A variation of this game would be to focus on ending consonant digraphs.

Steal the Bacon

In this version of the game, fourteen children are divided into two groups of seven each. The two groups stand about ten feet apart and face each other. An object, such as a beanbag, is placed in the center about five feet from each group. Each member of each group is given a letter; *b, c, d, h, m, n,* and *p,* as in the following diagram:

b		p
c		n
d		m
h	beanbag (bacon)	h
m		d
n		c
p		b

The teacher calls out a word such as *ball,* and the two children having the letter *b* run out to grab the beanbag. If the child gets the beanbag back to his line he scores two points for his group. If his opponent tags him before he gets back, the other group scores one point. The game continues in this manner.

Comment: This game helps the teacher see how well children can distinguish between beginning sounds. This activity is very useful as a means of diagnosing reading readiness because it is concerned with auditory discrimination of beginning consonants.

Rhythmic Activities

In Chapter 3 rhythmic activities were described as those human movement experiences that *require* some sort of rhythmical accompaniment. In view of the fact that children need to attend to relevant auditory cues in the form of rhythmical accompaniment for rhythmic activities, this seems to be an important place to comment on some of the various forms of accompaniment. Five forms of accompaniment for rhythmic activities are presented here, along with what might be considered as advantages and disadvantages of each.

1. *Clapping* as a form of accompaniment can be useful in helping children gain a better understanding of tempo. There is also something to be said for the child actually becoming part of the accompaniment on a physical basis, since it gives him a feeling that he is more involved. This is particularly important in the early stages when rhythmic activities are being introduced. Clapping can be done with the hands or by slapping various parts of the body such as the thighs or knees. A major disadvantage of clapping as a form of accompaniment is that it is virtually impossible to obtain a melody.

2. Various kinds of percussion instruments may be used as accompaniment, the most prominent being the *drum*. The drum, an easy-to-play instrument, offers the person furnishing the accompaniment the choice of changing tempo as he wishes. Actually, some kinds of dances, such as some of the Indian dances, require the use of a drum as accompaniment. As in the case of clapping, the use of a drum almost precludes a melody.

3. *Singing* as a form of accompaniment is ordinarily required in singing games and in square dances where singing calls are used. All children can become involved as in the case of clapping. One of the disadvantages of singing as a form of accompaniment is that the singing voices may become weaker as the child participates in the activity. For example,

if singing games require a great deal of skipping, it is difficult for the child to do both tasks of singing and skipping for a very long period of time.

4. At one time the *piano* was a very popular form of melodic accompaniment for rhythmic activities. The chief disadvantage of the piano is that it is a difficult instrument to learn to play and all teachers have not included it as a part of their professional preparation. Another disadvantage is that even though one is an accomplished pianist, the player must obviously be at the piano and therefore, away from the activity.

5. Perhaps the most popular form of accompaniment at the present time is *recordings.* Sources from which to obtain recordings are so plentiful that almost any kind of accompaniment is available. One distinct disadvantage of some recordings are the instructions furnished for children. Sometimes these instructions are confusing and too difficult for younger children to understand. The teacher should evaluate such instructions. If it is found that they are too difficult for a particular group of children to understand, the teacher can use only the musical accompaniment. However, teachers might consider using a recorder to tape their own music or singing voices of children as a form of accompaniment.

The various kinds of rhythmic activities provide opportunities for sound discrimination, auditory memory, and auditory figure-ground discrimination. As far as the latter is concerned, it is much like visual figure-ground operation in that one is able to detect one specific tonal quality and frequency range imbedded within a whole complexity of sound.[20] Problems may arise in the ability to follow verbal instructions given against a background of distracting environmental sounds. For example, in square dancing, the child must process the auditory input of the calls above the musical background.[21]

---

[20]Hope M. Smith, "Implications for Movement Education Experiences Drawn from Perceptual-Motor Research, *Journal of Health, Physical Education and Recreation,* April, 1970.

[21]Perceptual-Motor Learning Guidelines, Baltimore City Schools, Baltimore, Maryland, 1973.

The following example shows how training in sound discrimination and auditory memory can be accomplished through the use of *fundamental rhythms,* which are basic to other, more complex, rhythmic patterns. Almost any form of accompaniment can be used for the fundamental locomotor movements of walking, running, jumping, leaping, hopping, skipping, galloping and sliding.

An important factor in fundamental rhythms is that of *cadence.* Theoretically, this refers to the number of steps or paces taken over a period of time, or accompaniment tempo. If one were to have children perform the fundamental movement of walking to the accompaniment of a drum, this could be done at the tempo of four beats to a *measure* in 4-4 time. This is shown in the following score with *quarter* notes. The quarter note is referred to as a *walk* note.

Accompaniment for running is twice as fast and is depicted with *eighth* notes (*run* notes as in the following score).

Many different sequences of walking and running can be used by various beats as follows:

walk, walk, run

walk, walk, run, run, run

run, run, walk, run, run, walk

walk, walk, run, run, run, run

A walk and run note can be used together for the uneven fundamental rhythms of skipping, galloping, and sliding. The following score depicts the use of this for skipping (step-hop).

In addition to the drum accompaniment suggested above and controlled by the teacher, many records provide musical background accompaniment for the performance of various fundamental rhythms. The information presented here is merely suggestive, and the creative teacher, with the collaboration of the children, can develop many exciting aspects of fundamental rhythms appropriate for use in sound discrimination and auditory memory.

Self-testing Activities

One of the ways of providing for auditory-motor association in self-testing activities is the use of auditory input in the performance of stunt activities. For example, young children like to perform animal imitations. When they learn how to perform the various stunts the teacher can identify the stunts by name and have them change from one stunt to another by calling out the name of the stunt. Two examples of such animal imitations follow.

Puppy Dog Run

The child places his hands, palms flat and fingers forward, on the surface area in front of his feet. The hands should be under the shoulders for support. The child bends his legs slightly to allow his back to move parallel with the surface area. He then walks forward using both arms and both legs to mimic a running dog. The gait can be increased as the child becomes more proficient.

Elephant Walk

From an erect standing position, the child bends forward at the waist until his back is parallel with the surface area. His arms are straight and held beneath his shoulders. His legs remain straight throughout the walk. As the child steps slowly, he swings his arms from side to side. The swaying motion will resemble an elephant swinging its trunk as it walks.

Chapter 8

IMPLEMENTING COMPENSATORY PHYSICAL EDUCATION

R EGARDLESS of how promising any given theory might be, the fact remains that the true test of its value will be the extent to which it can be put into practice. The function of this final chapter will be to give consideration to several of those factors which are of importance to the implementation of compensatory physical education.

PROFESSIONAL PREPARATION

Obviously important factors in the implementation of any kind of endeavor are the qualifications of those persons who have the responsibility for carrying it out. Thus, perhaps one of the initial considerations is the professional preparation of individuals who will in some way work in the area of compensatory physical education. In view of the fact that this branch of physical education is concerned with improvement in learning ability as it is related to perceptual-motor deficiencies, we need to examine the extent to which professional preparation in this area is needed. An important step in this direction was taken by the Perceptual-Motor Task Force which was appointed by the Physical Education Division of the American Association for Health, Physical Education and Recreation in 1967. The content of the immediate discussion of this section of the chapter which follows has been derived from the publication produced by this group.[1]

It is considered essential that all physical educators, regardless

---

[1]Marguerite A. Clifton, "Nature and Extent of Professional Preparation Experiences in Perceptual-motor Development," *Foundations & Practices in Perceptual-motor Learning — A Quest for Understanding,* American Association for Health, Physical Education and Recreation (Washington, D. C., 1971): pp. 32-35.

of intended vocational direction, fully understand the neurological organization underlying learning, the anatomical and neural aspects of the sense organs pertinent to movement and their stages of development, and the role of perceptual organization in movement behavior. And further, that professional preparation in perceptual-motor development should: (1) be required of all students preparing to assume the role of teacher or researcher, (2) include the major conceptual areas required in understanding the processing of sensory information during the act of learning, (3) include the major concepts in learning categorized as affectors, and which are unique to each individual, (4) include the conceptual areas which would help the teacher to structure a most effective environment, and (5) examine assessment tools and their appropriate uses in evaluating the phases of a given learning situation.

Certainly this program, while a somewhat ambitious undertaking, is worthy of consideration. However, such detailed study as these recommendations imply is perhaps some years off. In the meantime, certain basic courses involving learning disability, its causes and contributing causes, should be incorporated into professional preparation programs. In addition, in-service activities intended to help teachers implement improvement of learning ability through compensatory physical education should be provided as needed.

THE TEACHER

The focal point of any teaching-learning situation is the teacher. The job of the teacher in any branch of physical education is a complex one. Many important competencies, abilities and experiences are needed by the teacher in order to provide physical education experiences in the most desirable way. The ensuing discussion will take into account certain factors of compensatory physical education concerned with (1) the special teacher of compensatory physical education, (2) the regular physical education teacher, (3) the classroom teacher, and (4) the special resource teacher of children with learning disabilities.

The Special Teacher

In this frame of reference the term *special teacher* refers to a special teacher of compensatory physical education. It is to be doubted that there will be many situations in which an individual will have such a title. This is due to the fact that the concept may be relatively new, and in addition, it is questionable whether there is a need for such a person. Schools have secured the services of a perceptual-motor specialist in a few, limited situations, and this specialist ordinarily operates within the framework of the physical education program. Until the time arrives when individuals can be prepared as special teachers of compensatory physical education, and until there is a great need for such personnel, this responsibility is likely to be assumed by the regular physical education teacher, with the assistance of the classroom teacher.

The Regular Physical Education Teacher

In general, there are two ways in which regular physical education teachers can utilize compensatory physical education methods. They may incorporate these routines within the framework of the regular physical education program and/or conduct special classes oriented to compensatory physical education.

When incorporating these types of experiences in the regular physical education program, the teacher must be alert to, and aware of, the perceptual-motor experiences inherent in the various activities. There are very few kinds of regular physical education activitities that do not involve some aspect of perceptual-motor development. It could be possible for the teacher to group children in such a way within the regular class so each of them could benefit from certain aspects of perceptual-motor training.

It could be possible for the teacher, with the assistance of the principal, to schedule special classes with a compensatory physical education orientation. Presently, some physical education teachers are teaching such classes within the framework of the special education program.

The Classroom Teacher

Getting the classroom teacher involved in compensatory physical education presents some of the same problems as getting this individual to participate in the regular curricular physical education program. The interest of the classroom teacher in the endeavor of compensatory physical education must be obtained. Perhaps the initiative in this direction might be taken by the physical education teacher. Presently, the trend toward *mainstreaming* children with learning disabilities has placed the responsibility for program development for the mildly and moderately learning impaired on the classroom teacher. When classroom teachers are able to see that compensatory physical education has a possible capability to improve learning ability, and thus facilitate learning, they will be more likely to want to contribute to this effort.

There is a relatively new development which encourages the classroom teacher to cooperate in a compensatory physical education program. This is what has become known as the *Open Classroom*. Under the supervision of the physical education teacher, learning centers and stations can be set up in the classroom, and necessary equipment can be provided. The program has often met with success in schools where the open classroom structure exists.

The Special Resource Teacher

An emerging special educator role is that of the resource teacher who is providing support to the learning impaired children *mainstreamed* into regular classes. The special resource teacher is competent to assist teachers to set goals and to make appropriate curricular and methodological decisions. A possibility that should be explored is that the compensatory physical education teacher, the regular physical education teacher, the special resource teacher, and the classroom teacher function as a team to plan and provide specific developmental activities for children's perceptual-motor needs. Skills in assessment of learning abilities and disabilities of individual students, planning learning activities for children with perceptual-motor needs and academic and social needs can be shared by the educators in the school setting.

The special resource teacher can be a very important functionary in compensatory physical education, either by working independently or in cooperation with the physical education teacher. An important facet of the role played by the special resource teacher would be working with specific cases in which there may be a pronounced degree of perceptual-motor deficiency. The individual activities, in the form of the self-testing activities suggested in the text, can be very useful where the special resource teacher works with such cases on an individual basis.

OUT-OF-SCHOOL PROGRAMS

Out-of-school programs of the general nature of compensatory physical education have met with varying degrees of success. Oftentimes this type of program will be under the sponsorship of a local university. Such an example is the exemplary Children's Health and Developmental Clinic at the University of Maryland. The clinic was organized by its present director, Dr. Warren R. Johnson. It should be mentioned that Dr. Johnson uses the term *clinical* physical education, which he introduced to the literature in the mid-1960s.[2] The clinic was organized in the spring of 1957 in response to a growing need in the Washington, D. C., area for a program specializing in improving the physical fitness and/or coordination of subfit children. Under the leadership of the Director, volunteer student clinicians are trained to work with children referred from a variety of agencies and organizations. The clinic's agenda involves a wide variety of gymnasium activities, conditioning and coordination exercises, games, and modified sports; they are much the same as many of the activities recommended in this text. A number of similar clinics have "spun off" from the parent clinic and are being operated at various institutions around the country by former students of Dr. Johnson.

---

[2]Warren R. Johnson and Richard Hendricks, "Management of Speech Handicaps in Clinical Physical Education, *The Journal of the Association for Physical and Mental Rehabilitation,* March-April, 1965.

The suggestions and recommendations given in this final chapter for the implementation of compensatory physical education have met with varying degrees of success. The main point of concern is that if there is any validity to the approach as far as the improvement of learning ability is concerned, then positive efforts should be made in this direction to facilitate learning for children.

AUTHOR INDEX

145

SUBJECT INDEX

147